WINDOWS™ 3.

QUICK START

Marly Bergerud
Dean, Business Science Division
Saddleback College

Don Busché, Ed. D.
Dean, Vocational Education
Saddleback College

SOUTH-WESTERN PUBLISHING CO.

Acquisitions Editor:	Randy R. Sims
Consulting Editor:	Margaret Cheatham
Editorial Production Manager:	Linda R. Allen
Production Editor:	Daniel E. Van
Associate Editor:	Timothy J. Bailey
Designer:	Elaine St. John-Lagenaur
Production Artist:	Steven McMahon
Marketing Manager:	Brian Taylor

Copyright © 1993

by South-Western Publishing Co.

Cincinnati, Ohio

2 3 4 5 6 7 8 9 H 00 99 98 97 96 95 94 93 92

Printed in the United States of America

Bergerud, Marly
    Windows 3 : quick start / Marly Bergerud, Don Busche.
      p.   cm.
    Includes index.
    ISBN 0-538-70849-2
    1. Windows (Computer programs) 2. Microsoft Windows (Computer program)   I. Busche, Don.   II. Title.
QA76.76.W56B44   1992
005.4 ' 3--dc20   91-48347
                                                              CIP

CONTENTS

CONTENTS

INTRODUCTION: WHAT IS WINDOWS?

Perhaps you're wondering about the name **Windows**. A very simple name. The name of something we are all familiar with. Certainly not a "technical" or a difficult name. Yet Windows is, as you will see, an accurate name for this software program.

As you use Windows, each "view" lets you communicate with your computer by simply pointing at images you see. Each image, called an **icon**, is a little picture or symbol that identifies a closed window, a window you can open and use for a special purpose. Together, the icons and the windows they represent make up the desktop, an offering of choices that will let you tell the computer what you want in the easiest way. Just as you choose from icons, you also choose from menus, which give you lists of options. With Windows, all you do to make a choice is point at an icon, a menu, or an option.

Your pointer is a mouse, a small device that fits in the palm of your hand. Because the mouse sits on a ball, you can roll the mouse on your tabletop. As you roll the mouse, you move the pointer on the screen. The mouse is a quick way of letting you point to icons, menus, and options without using the keyboard.

If you are familiar with computers, you know that in the past you had to memorize, remember, and finally key a variety of difficult system (DOS, or disk operating system) commands in order to direct the computer to perform various actions. With Windows, you will not encounter difficult commands, yet you will be able to perform the same kinds of tasks, use a variety of familiar software programs, organize your hard disk, and more.

In place of difficult commands, Windows icons offer you a selection of easy-to-understand symbols (in color if you have a color monitor). And Windows menus offer you a few simple words. The result: Using your computer is easier because you understand what you must do, and at the same time you have more fun and get greater satisfaction. Perhaps best of all, you use menus and menu options the same way in every piece of Windows software, so you don't have to learn different commands for each new program! You can play games, send messages, set an alarm clock, draw pictures, schedule your day, create a picture calendar, even customize Windows to make each window appear the way you want. How? Again, by choosing from icons and menus.

Perhaps you now understand that Windows creates a visual relationship between you and your computer called a **graphical environment**. From this visual setting, you choose familiar images that represent office applications, instead of memorizing difficult commands. This new, easier way to work with computers is called a **graphical user interface** (for short, **GUI**, pronounced "gooey").

Why is the GUI environment important? Because it provides one consistent way of using—and switching between—many different programs. For example, in this GUI environment you can use programs that come with Windows, such as Write, Paintbrush, and Cardfile. Plus, you can use hundreds of other popular programs such as WordPerfect and Lotus 1-2-3.

Naming Conventions

You will find this book easier to read and understand if you know how it treats special terms. In this book:

- The word **Windows** refers to the software program "Windows™ 3" (created by Microsoft® Corporation).

- Capital letters and brackets in bold type identify function keys and other labeled keys; for example:

  [F3]   [F9]   [Backspace]

  [Enter]   [Spacebar]

- When you must press two (or more) keys at the same time, the keys will be shown in brackets with a plus sign; for example: **[Alt]** + **[F]**.

- The names of menus and menu options, commands, and dialog boxes are capitalized; for example:

  the Help menu
  the Print option
  the Save As... command
  the Save As dialog box

- The word "key" is used whenever you must type information on the keyboard.

Note: A set of three dots following a command name indicates that a dialog box will follow.

- Italics identify characters that you must key:

  Key *Word Processing* in the Description text box...

A Word About System Requirements

The suggested minimum computer hardware requirements for Windows 3 are:

- IBM® or IBM-compatible PC

- 80286 or 80386 microprocessor

- 4 to 7 Mb RAM (temporary memory)

- MS-DOS® version 3.1 or higher

- One hard disk (6 to 8Mb free)

- One 3½ or 5¼-inch disk drive

- A graphics display or monitor (Hercules®-compatible video card)
- An enhanced keyboard
- A mouse or pen pointer
- A dot matrix printer

Again, these are the suggested minimum requirements. If your system has only an 8088 or 8086 microprocessor, Windows will run too slowly. Having less than 4 Mb of RAM is not wise because of the large amount of memory required when running a number of programs at one time. While a mouse is not essential (every menu lists keyboard commands), a mouse greatly increases efficiency and productivity. A color monitor (CGA, EGA, or VGA) and a laser printer are nice to have but not essential.

Ready, Set, ...

Windows 3: Quick Start is a friendly, step-by-step book. Each Session is divided into Views. Each View discusses new concepts in the Preview section and provides activities in the Exercise section.

 When you should be using your computer to complete an exercise, you will see this icon in the margin. Otherwise, you should be reading text (as in the Preview, for example).

Before you begin with Session 1, make sure that Windows has been installed on your hard drive (usually drive C). Further, make sure that you have received specific instructions for saving your completed work, and that you have a high-density floppy disk available for data storage.

...Go!

• • • • • • • • • • • •

OBJECTIVES

When you complete this session, you will be able to:

- Define basic terms such as *system prompt*, *desktop*, *window screens*, *icons*, *title bar*, *menu bar*, *mouse*, and *mouse pointer*.

- Use a mouse to pull down menus, select icons, and issue commands.

- Recognize on-screen pointers and explain their meaning.

- Practice using keyboard shortcuts.

- Work with menus, menu bars, dialog boxes, and messages.

- Open, close, and control the size and the location of windows.

- Utilize the Windows Help system.

- Start, close, and exit Windows.

SESSION 1

EXPLORING WINDOWS

• • • • • • • • • • • • • •

EXPLORING WINDOWS

▼ ▲

VIEW 1
STARTING WINDOWS

PREVIEW

Before you begin, do you know where the Windows program resides in your computer? For most computers, Windows will be located on drive C. For some computers, the Windows program may be on drive D. Where is it on your computer system?

As you start to use Windows, remember what you have read about its graphical environment. As you work through each view in this Quick Start, you will be reinforcing *one consistent* way of performing common tasks for different programs within Windows.

EXERCISE 1 ● 1   STARTING WINDOWS

Look at Figure 1.1, the Opening Screen of the Windows Desktop. The **desktop**, the overall work area on the screen, is the Windows equivalent of the top surface of your desk. You put things on your desk, take things off your desk, and move things around on your desk. In the same way, you will place items on, remove items from, and move items around your desktop.

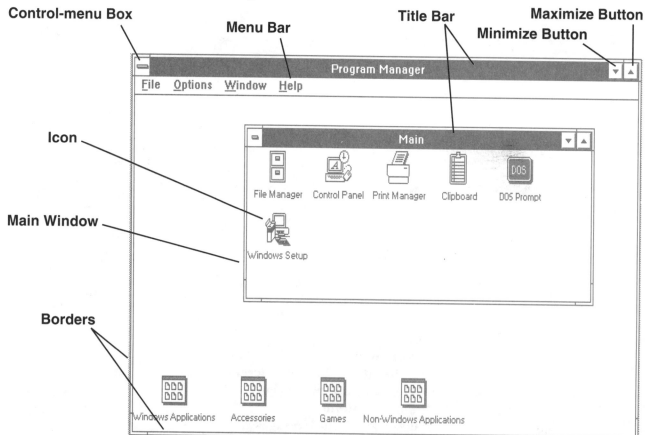

Figure 1.1 Opening screen

Now let's look closer at your Windows opening screen and Figure 1.1.

1. If necessary, start your Windows program by keying *WIN* **[Enter]** at the system prompt. (Remember that brackets **[ ]** indicate the name of a specific key. Therefore, you should key the text "WIN" and press the **[Enter]** key.)

2. Compare your screen with the one illustrated in Figure 1.1. The appearance of your screen may differ sightly from the one illustrated, but the basic elements should be the same. Do you see a **title bar** as shown in Figure 1.1? A **menu bar**? Spend a few minutes looking at the layout of the screen and the position of these elements—the boxes, the symbols, the words. Remember, there may be slight differences. If your screen does not display elements similar to those shown in Figure 1.1, ask for assistance.

VIEW 2
EXAMINING THE WINDOWS SCREEN

PREVIEW

At first sight, the Windows screen in Figure 1.1 may look rather complicated because it contains a variety of symbols and words that are now meaningless to you. A closer look will *un*complicate this screen and make the elements clear and understandable. Then, because all the other screens follow the same basic format and have the same parts, you will have no trouble using the many different options Windows has to offer.

To begin, just look at the opening screen as two windows: The Program Manager window and the Main window.

The Program Manager Window

The words *Program Manager* appear on the first line of the Program Manager window. As shown in Figure 1.1, this darkened part of the first line is called a **title bar**. The title bar contains the name of the application running in a window. Directly below the title bar is a **menu bar**. The menu bar is a list of choices, and the specific choices depend upon the application you are running. For instance, the Program Manager menu bar offers these four choices: File   Options   Window   Help

The Main Window

Within the Program Manager window sits the Main window. Look again at Figure 1.1. Find the word *Main* in the title bar at the top of the Main window. Then look at the small images or pictures in the Main window. These small images, called **icons**, appear often.

The Main window, with its icons, is shown in Figure 1.1. Each icon represents a choice of a different window or a different application you can use. We will discuss icons and the choices they represent in greater detail later.

Other Elements of the Windows Screen

In addition to icons, title bars, and menu bars, you need to know about some other window elements. Again, look at Figure 1.1, noting the labels that show various elements of the Program Manager window. Then read the following explanations of those elements:

- The **Control-menu box** lies in the upper-left corner of the Program Manager window, on the same line as the title bar. In this box is a short line; it looks like a dash. This box opens the Control menu, which offers you options for "controlling" the size of the window displays or moving elements within the window displays.

- The **minimize and maximize buttons** are at the upper-right corner, also on the same line as the title bar. The minimize button reduces the window to an icon, and the maximize button enlarges the window to fill the screen.

- The **borders** are the four lines that define the limits of the window. Later you will see how to enlarge and reduce the size of a window by moving its borders.

As soon as you learn to move around the screen, you will better understand the above explanations.

VIEW 3
MOVING AROUND THE SCREEN

PREVIEW

Question: How do you move around the Windows screen? Answer: With a mouse, or with a keyboard. The keyboard lets you crawl around, step by step. The mouse lets you race all over the screen—and if you want, carry materials with you as you move!

Using the Mouse

The mouse is an input device that allows you to find, move to, and grab any tools or files you need to place on your desktop; you can also use the mouse to put those tools or files away. The mouse serves a number of other convenient uses, which will be discussed later. Your desktop is a visual work area, and the mouse is the key to that work area. Once you use and feel comfortable with the mouse, you'll know why Windows works more effectively when you use a mouse.

The Mouse Pointer. The mouse controls an on-screen pointer in the shape of an arrow (see Figure 1.2). To move the pointer up or down, to the left or to the right, just slide the mouse. When you get "cornered," that is, when you run out of room on your real desk, you can lift the mouse off your desk, move the mouse, and then set it back down—all without moving the on-screen pointer.

The on-screen pointer changes its appearance. Depending on where you are on the screen and what you are doing, the pointer will change to look like an hourglass, a crosshair, or a pointing finger. Figure 1.3 shows some of the shapes the pointer can assume.

The Mouse Buttons. So, the mouse lets you move around the screen quickly, but what do you do when you "get there?" Besides moving the pointer around the screen, the mouse allows you to move windows and choose various applications. How? By using mouse **buttons**.

Figure 1.2

Mouse and on-screen pointer

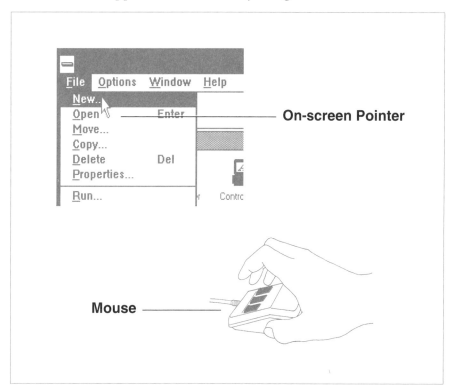

Figure 1.3

Each of these on-screen pointers has its own unique message.

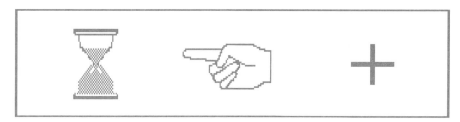

Every mouse has one, two, or three buttons, depending on the particular brand (the left button is the one you will use most often). Pressing and then releasing a mouse button is referred to as **clicking**; for some commands, you will need to **double-click** (that is, click twice quickly). You'll learn exactly what to do, and when to do it, as you practice using Windows. Figure 1.4 lists different techniques of using a mouse.

Dragging With the Mouse. In addition to moving the pointer, the mouse can also be used to move objects or icons around the screen. Moving objects with the mouse is known as **dragging**. You "drag" an object by placing the mouse pointer on the item to be moved and then pressing and *holding down the mouse button* while moving the object. When the pointer is at the right location, release the mouse button. That's all there is to dragging.

Using the mouse requires a little practice; soon you will become comfortable—and proficient—in using it. Just be patient.

Figure 1.4

Mouse techniques

Mouse Techniques

To	Do this:
Drag	Press the mouse button and move the mouse in the desired direction.
Click	Press and release the mouse button.
Select	Point on and click the mouse button.
Double Click	Click twice in rapid succession on the mouse button.

EXERCISE 1 • 2   USING THE MOUSE

1. Move the mouse around the desktop (or mouse pad, if you have one) and watch the screen to see how the pointer moves.

   a. Move the pointer to the far left of your screen by sliding the mouse to the left on the desktop or mouse pad. Do not lift the mouse.

   b. Move the pointer to the far right of your screen by sliding the mouse to the right.

   c. Move the pointer to the top of your screen by moving the mouse toward the top of your desktop.

   d. Move the pointer to the bottom of your screen by moving the mouse toward the bottom of your desktop or mouse pad.

2. Display and close the Control menu box.

   a. Point to the Control menu box in the upper-left corner of the Program Manager window.

   b. Click (press and release) the mouse button.

   c. Compare your screen with the one illustrated in Figure 1.5.

   d. Point on the Control menu box and click the mouse button. The menu window should close.

3. Display and close each of the Program Manager menus.

   a. Display the File menu by pointing on the word "File" on the Program Manager menu bar and clicking the mouse button.

   b. Display the Options menu by pointing on the word "Options" on the Program Manager menu bar and clicking the mouse button. Did you notice that when you selected the new menu, the previously selected menu window was closed and the new window was displayed?

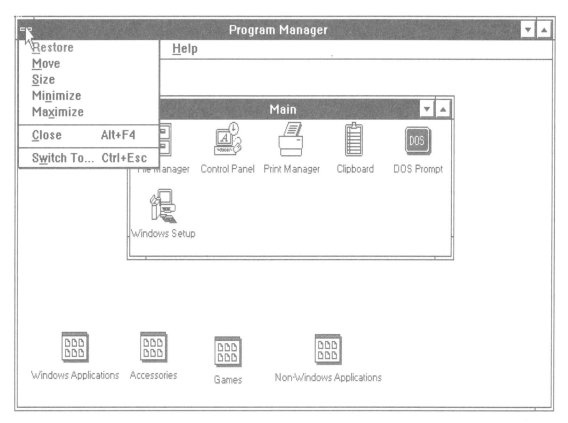

Figure 1.5   Control menu displayed over Program Manager and Main windows

    c. Display each of the remaining Program Manager menus by pointing and clicking on them one at a time.

4. If icons are displayed at the bottom of the Program Manager window, display the menu of each of the icons.

    a. Point on the far-left icon and click the mouse button.

    b. Point on the icon to the right of the one you just clicked on. Notice that when you selected the new icon, the previously selected menu was closed and the new icon menu was displayed.

    c. Display each of the remaining icon menus by pointing and clicking on each icon one at a time.

    d. Click on any clear area on the screen to close the displayed menu.

5. Rearrange the order of the icons on the desktop.

    a. Point on the icon you wish to move first. While holding down on the mouse button, drag the icon to the desired location and release the mouse button. Place the icon slightly above the current row of icons near the position you want it to appear.

    b. Point on the next icon to be repositioned, and drag the icon to the desired location.

    c. Continue to drag the icons until they appear in the desired sequence.

Using the Keyboard

Whether you have a mouse or not, you can use the keyboard to perform most of the same functions that the mouse performs. In fact, many windows tell you which keystrokes to use as an alternate to using the mouse. These **keyboard shortcuts**, as they are called, often use a combination of keys (usually the **[Alt]** key or the **[Ctrl]** key with some other key).

For example, the keyboard shortcut to display the Program Manager File menu is **[Alt]** + **[F]**. Using the **[F]** for "File" makes this combination easy to remember. The other Program Manager menu shortcuts also combine **[Alt]** with an underscored letter on the menu bar.

In the following exercises, the keyboard shortcuts will be indicated in their short form, that is, capitalized and enclosed in brackets. For example, you will see **[F1]**, **[F2]**, etc., for the function keys and **[Tab]**, **[Shift]**, etc., for the labeled keys. When you are to press two or more keys simultaneously, these keys are shown with a plus symbol between them; for example, **[Alt]** + **[F]**. When you must issue two keyboard shortcuts, one after the other, the word *then* will separate the shortcuts. For example, the keyboard shortcuts **Alt** key, **F** key and **Control** key, **W** key are written **[Alt]** + **[F]** then **[Control]** + **[W]**.

EXERCISE 1 ● 3   USING KEYBOARD SHORTCUTS

1. Display each of the Program Manager menus using the keyboard shortcut.

    a. Display the File menu **[Alt]** + **[F]**. Release the keys once the menu is displayed.

    b. Display the Options menu **[Alt]** + **[O]**. Did you notice that in each case, the keyboard shortcut consisted of holding down the **Alt** key and pressing the letter underscored on the menu bar?

    c. Display the Windows menu **[Alt]** + **[W]**.

    d. Display the Help menu **[Alt]** + **[H]**.

2. Close the displayed menu by pressing **[Esc]**.

Clearly, Windows works best with a mouse; therefore, **all future instructions assume you are using a mouse**. Of course, whenever you want to use a keyboard shortcut, you'll find it on the appropriate pull-down menu. They are also listed in the back of this book.

▬	VIEW 4	▼ ▲
	MENUS AND MENU BARS	

PREVIEW

Earlier, you learned that a **menu** is a list of options or choices. Now you will see and work with menus.

If all menus were on your desktop at the same time, your work area would be too cluttered to be useful. Windows' menus are out of sight but within reach: You can easily pull down a menu and find what you want.

In the last exercise, when you displayed the various Program Manager menus, did you notice that each menu contained different options? That's how you will issue commands—by choosing from menu options. To make your choice, select an option from the menu bar. Then look at the menu bar, point at the option you want, and click the mouse button. As you click, you will "pull down" another menu from the menu bar. A pull-down menu is shown in Figure 1.6.

When you see the pull-down menu, select one of the options listed. Again, look at the pull-down menu, point at the option you want, and then click the mouse button. Your command will be executed.

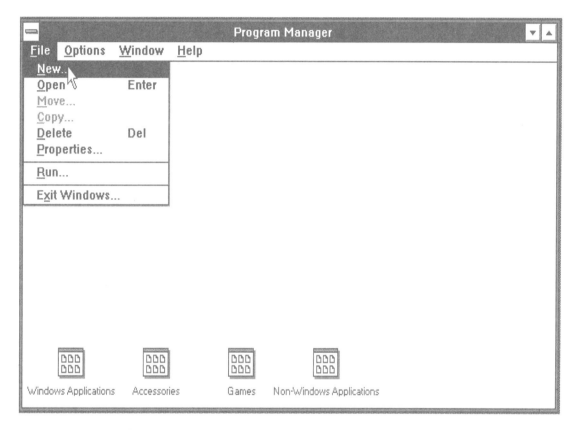

Figure 1.6 Program Manager window with File menu displayed and first option highlighted

Window Screen Elements

If you look closely at Figure 1.6, you will notice some differences in how options appear. Some are highlighted, some are in dark black print, some are followed by ellipsis points (...), but all have one letter underlined. All these visual elements have special meanings, as explained below.

HIGHLIGHTING

The first menu option is highlighted. **Highlighting** means that the words appear in white letters within a black box and indicates that this option is currently "selected." If you wish to select a different option, point and click on the desired option. Use the **[Up Arrow]** and **[Down Arrow]** keys to move the black highlight box up and down the menu list. When you click the mouse button, the highlighted option becomes selected.

COLOR   Not all menu options are available to you. The dark or black print indicates options that are currently available. Light or grayish print indicates options that are not available. Look closely at the File menu in Figure 1.6. How many of its options are currently available? (Answer: six.)

ELLIPSIS   A series of three periods (...), called an **ellipsis**, appears to the right of some menu options. An ellipsis tells you that if you choose this option, a second window will be displayed, requesting more information from you.

KEYBOARD SHORTCUTS   Each menu option has one underscored letter or number, indicating a keyboard shortcut. This keyboard shortcut can only be used while the menu is displayed. To use a shortcut from a specific menu option, press its underscored letter or number.

EXERCISE 1 ● 4   WORKING WITH MENUS

1. Display the Help menu.

   a. Select the About Program Manager option by pressing the letter **[A]**.

   b. Close the window by clicking on OK or pressing **[Enter]**.

2. Select the Accessories option from the Windows menu. Did you notice that the Accessories window was added to the Program Manager window?

3. Select the Games option from the Windows menu.

4. Select the Tile option from the Windows menu or use the keyboard shortcut (**[Shift]** + **[F4]**). The windows are now arranged differently; they are arranged in a tiled format.

5. Select the Cascade option from the Windows menu (or use the keyboard shortcut **[Shift]** + **[F5]**). The tiled windows now return to the cascade format.

VIEW 5

DIALOG BOXES AND MESSAGES

PREVIEW

Figure 1.7

File menu

File	
New..	
Open	Enter
Move...	
Copy...	
Delete	Del
Properties...	
Run...	
Exit Windows...	

Some menu options, like many on the File menu (Figure 1.7), need more information before they can be executed. For example, before Windows can run (start) a program, it needs to know the program name. When an option needs additional information before the command can be executed, the menu option is followed by an ellipsis (...) (see Figure 1.7). How does it get that information? It does so in the form of a **dialog box**, which is shown in Figure 1.8.

A dialog box is itself a window. For example, when you select the Run... option, you'll see the Run dialog box (illustrated in Figure 1.8). When you select the Properties... option, you'll see the Properties dialog box.

Figure 1.8

Run dialog box from the File menu

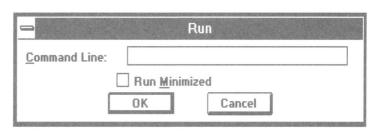

Dialog Box Elements

Now that you know how dialog boxes are named, take a look at the elements you will find in dialog boxes—buttons and boxes.

There are two types of buttons—command buttons and option buttons.

COMMAND BUTTON

Figure 1.9

Command buttons carry out your instructions, using the information selected in the dialog box. Command buttons are always rectangles. When you press a command button, the program accepts your instructions and the dialog box closes.

OPTION BUTTON

Figure 1.10

Option buttons allow you to choose one option from a group. You may change your selection by choosing a different button.

There are four types of boxes—check boxes, list boxes, text boxes, and drop-down list boxes.

CHECK BOX

Figure 1.11

Check boxes also allow you to make choices from a group. However, unlike an option button, you can check more than one box to select a variety of options. When there is an X in the box, the option is selected. Clicking with the mouse selects or deselects a check box.

LIST BOX

Figure 1.12

Files:

| ansi.sys |
| append.exe |
| assign.com |
| attrib.exe |
| backup.com |
| basic.com |
| basic.pif |
| basica.com |
| basica.pif |

List boxes are found in both windows and dialog boxes. Often, a list of items is too lengthy to fit in a box. In such cases, scroll bars are used to allow you to scroll through the items. Items are arranged alphabetically.

TEXT BOX

Figure 1.13

Text boxes are found in dialog boxes and as part of Windows applications. A text box is an area in which you can key in information. A blinking insertion point shows you where your keyed text will be displayed. You can move the insertion point with a mouse click. If the box already has text, the previous text will be highlighted and will automatically erase when you begin to key in text. To work with text in a text box, you will need to select it. Text that is selected appears in a different color, usually white text on a black background.

DROP-DOWN LIST BOX

Figure 1.14

A drop-down list box lists only one option and a special arrow symbol. Click on the arrow symbol to reveal the entire list box.

EXERCISE 1 • 5   DIALOG BOXES AND MESSAGES

1. Select Run... from the File menu. This dialog box contains a text box, a check box, and two command buttons (see Figure 1.8).

2. Key your first name in the text box—do not press **[Enter]**. Notice the blinking cursor where you are to begin keying.

3. Click on the Run Minimize check box. Notice that the item is checked (selected).

4. Click on the OK command button. You now see a message box similar to the one illustrated in Figure 1.15. This message box is displayed to communicate with you. In this case, Windows is telling you that it cannot locate the file you asked it to run. Later we will run files using the Run dialog box, but for now let's cancel our instruction.

5. Click on the OK command button.

6. Click on the Cancel command button to cancel the Run command.

Figure 1.15

A message box

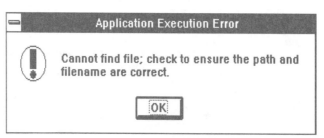

VIEW 6
GETTING HELP

PREVIEW

If you need assistance while working in Windows, use Windows Help, a built-in help facility designed to provide you with information about Windows and its applications. The Windows Help facility looks and acts the same in each application, but the information is specific to that application.

The Help text files are divided into eight main categories: Index, Keyboard, Basic Skills, Commands, Procedures, Glossary, and Using Help.

To access Help, select Help from an application's menu bar (almost every menu bar has one). Locate the Help menu on the Program Manager menu bar. You will be working with this menu later in this session.

Figure 1.16

Help menu bar

Different menu bars give different types of Help. Each Help menu has a list of categories similar to the ones shown in Figure 1.16. When chosen, each category displays a Help window with information about that category. Some applications may have different categories in the menu, depending on the nature of the application. You may also see a Help button in dialog boxes, as in Figure 1.17.

Figure 1.17

Help button

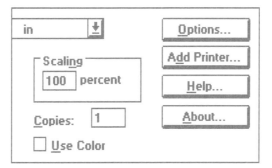

Whenever you choose a category from a Help menu, or choose a Help button, a Help window is displayed, as shown in Figure 1.18. Notice the buttons near the top of the Help window (Index, Back, Browse, and Search). These buttons help you navigate through the Help system.

Figure 1.18

Help window

Navigation buttons

In the Help text, you will notice that the underlined words are cross references and that words with a broken underline are terms. When you move the pointer over the underlined words, the pointer changes from an arrow to a hand icon. Selecting a cross reference will take you to a screen with information about that reference. To select a cross reference, point to the word and click.

Selecting a term will display a small box with a definition or short description (Figure 1.19). Selecting a term will not advance you to

Figure 1.19

Help term description

> **scroll bar**
>
> A bar that appears at the right and/or bottom edge of a window whose contents aren't completely visible. Each scroll bar contains two scroll arrows and a scroll box, which allow you to scroll within the window or list box.

another screen. To select a term, point to the word, press and hold the mouse button, and release the mouse button when you are finished viewing the information.

EXERCISE 1 • 6   USING THE HELP SYSTEM

The Browse Button

1. Select the Index option from the Program Manager Help menu. The Help window will be displayed.

2. Click three times on the Browse >> button. Notice that the subjects displayed in the Help window change each time you click on the button. When you click on the Browse >> button, you scan forward through the help text.

3. Click once on the Browse << button. When you click on the Browse << button, you scan backwards through the help text.

4. Point on the underscored words "scroll bar" (green words if you have a color monitor). (*Hint:* The words "scroll bar" are in the short paragraph entitled "Program Manager Help Index.") If the text is not displayed on the screen, use the Browse >> or the Browse << button to locate the words "scroll bar."

5. Select the underscored text, "scroll bar." A definition of *scroll bar* will be displayed as long as you hold down the mouse button.

Figure 1.20

Help Search dialog box

```
┌─────────────────────────────────────────────────────┐
│ ▄                        Search                       │
│  Search For:                                          │
│  ┌──────────────────────────────────────┐  ┌────────┐│
│  │active window                          │  │ Search ││
│  └──────────────────────────────────────┘  └────────┘│
│  ┌──────────────────────────────────────┐▲ ┌────────┐│
│  │active window                          │█ │ Cancel ││
│  │adding                                 │█ └────────┘│
│  │applications                           │█           │
│  │arranging                              │            │
│  │associate                              │            │
│  │Auto Arrange                           │▼           │
│  └──────────────────────────────────────┘            │
│  ─────────────────────────────────────────           │
│  No Topics Found                            ┌────────┐│
│                                             │ Go To  ││
│  ┌──────────────────────────────────────┐  └────────┘│
│  │                                       │            │
│  │                                       │            │
│  │                                       │            │
│  └──────────────────────────────────────┘            │
└─────────────────────────────────────────────────────┘
```

The Search Button

Clicking on the Search button will open a dialog box (see Figure 1.20). Once you key a word or phrase in the text box and click on the Search button, the help text will be searched and the topic you have requested will be displayed.

6. You should still have the Help window displayed on your screen. Click on the Search button.

7. Key the topic *Closing* in the text box.

8. Click on the Search button in the dialog box to begin the search.

Three topics will be listed in the list box at the bottom of the Search dialog box. You can move to any one of these topics and have the appropriate text displayed in the Help window by clicking on the Go To box or by double-clicking on any one of the topics.

9. Double-click on the Closing Dialog Boxes topic (second topic in the list box).

Notice that the corresponding text is displayed. When a window is too small to show all of its contents, scroll bars will be displayed so you can scroll the text into view (Figure 1.21).

Figure 1.21

Help window with scroll bars

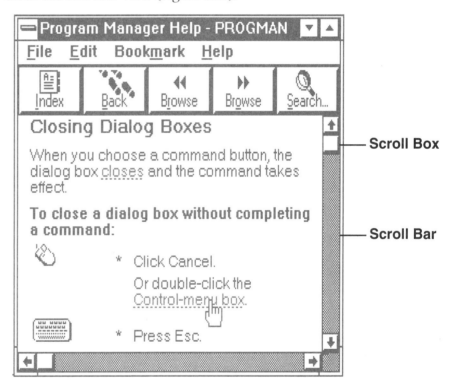

Scrolling the Help Text

To scroll a document, you can click on the up or down scroll arrow. Each time you click on the scroll arrow, the text will scroll up or down one line (depending on which arrow you use). If you continue to hold the mouse button down while pointing on a scroll arrow, the text will continue to scroll.

The scroll bar also has a scroll box. You can move through the text quickly by dragging the scroll bar to a position that corresponds approximately with the location you want to view. For example, if you want to view the middle of the text, move the scroll box to the middle of the scroll bar.

EXERCISE 1 • 7 SCROLLING THE HELP TEXT

1. Point on the down arrow on the vertical scroll bar and click once. Notice the text scrolls up one line.

2. Point on the down arrow on the vertical scroll bar and click once again.

3. Point on the down arrow on the vertical scroll bar and hold down the mouse button until the scroll box reaches the bottom of the vertical scroll bar. You should now be viewing the bottom (last) line of the text.

4. Point on the scroll box, press and hold down the mouse button, drag the scroll box to the middle of the scroll bar, and release the mouse button. (The scroll box won't actually move to the location of the pointer until you release the mouse button.) Notice the text moves up several lines.

5. Point on the up arrow on the vertical scroll bar and click once. Notice the text scrolls down one line.

6. Point on the up arrow on the vertical scroll bar and hold down the mouse button until the scroll box reaches the top of the vertical scroll bar. The top of the text is now again in view.

VIEW 7
CLOSING AND EXITING WINDOWS

PREVIEW

When you have finished working with a window and no longer need it on your desktop, you should close it. A window can be closed in four ways:

- Double-click on the Control menu box,
- Select Close from the Control menu,
- Press **[Ctrl]** + **[F4]**, or
- Select Exit Windows... from the File menu.

When you select Exit Windows... from the File menu, you close the Program Manager, and when you close the Program Manager, you also close all active windows and quit Windows.

EXERCISE 1 • 8 CLOSING A WINDOW

1. Click on the Help window to select it.

2. Click once on the Control menu; then select the Close option. The Help window will close.

3. Repeat steps *1* and *2* for the Games window.

4. Click on the Accessories window to select it.

5. Double-click on the Control menu. You must double-click quickly for the command to take effect. The Accessories window will close and its icon will appear at the bottom of the desktop.

6. Click on the Main window to select it.

7. Press and hold down the **[Ctrl]** key; then press the **[F4]** key. The Main window will close and its icon will appear at the bottom of the desktop.

Exiting Windows

Exiting Windows is a two-step process. First, you should close any programs you have been running in the Windows session. As with any application software package, closing an application before you turn off the computer will guard against losing current work. Second, once you have closed all applications that have been running, you close the Program Manager.

To end a Windows session, select the Exit Windows... command from the File menu in the Program Manager. Each time you exit (quit) Windows, the prompt box shown in Figure 1.22 will be displayed. The

Figure 1.22

Exit Windows prompt box

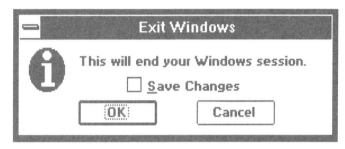

prompt box asks you to verify that you want to quit Windows and provides you with an opportunity to save the current

desktop layout of the Program Manager. If you check the Save Changes check box, the next time you open Windows, the icons and windows will be displayed as they were when you exited Windows. If you do not check the Save Changes check box, the Program Manager's workspace will be the same as it was the last time you launched Windows.

EXERCISE 1 ● 9 EXITING WINDOWS

1. Select the Exit Windows option from the File menu. The Exit Windows prompt box will appear.

2. Verify that the Save Changes check box is **not** checked. If it is checked, click on the check box to toggle the Save Changes option off.

3. Click on OK to exit Windows.

When you exit Windows, you return to the DOS prompt.

SUMMARY

In this introduction to Windows, you discovered basic terms, looked at some of the beginning procedures used to navigate in the Windows environment, and learned how to modify the appearance of the Windows workspace or desktop. You also learned how to access and use the Windows Help feature. The exercises provided practice in working with menus, menu bars, dialog boxes, and messages. You will use these features in the remaining sessions of this book as you continue working in the Windows environment.

• • • • • • • • • • • • •

OBJECTIVES

When you complete this session, you will be able to:

- Discuss the purpose and function of the Program Manager.

- Describe several programs in the Main group window that help you manage the Windows environment.

- Organize group windows and application program icons.

- Customize the Program Manager by copying, moving, and adding program icons and group windows.

- Switch between groups and create a new group window.

- Minimize, maximize, and restore group windows.

- Arrange windows and group items.

- Delete program items and a group.

- Start and quit an application and exit Windows.

SESSION 2

• • • • • • • • • • • • • • •
THE PROGRAM MANAGER

VIEWS
Group Windows
Working with Groups
Running Programs

THE PROGRAM MANAGER

● ● ● ● ● ● ● ● ● ● ● ● ● ● ● ●

GROUP WINDOWS

PREVIEW

The first thing you see when you begin Windows is the Program Manager window (see Figure 2.1), which appears automatically each time you begin a Windows session and remains open while Windows is running. The Program Manager allows you to control your programs and files. It's a utility, a tool that allows you to take full advantage of Windows. And as you will see later, you must use the Program Manager both to start Windows and to exit Windows.

NOTE: Each time you begin to work on Windows and you start up Windows software, your screen may not match exactly the ones shown in the textbook exercises and figures. In fact, throughout the *Windows Quick Start*, your actual screen displays may vary from the ones shown in the textbook. The differences are due to the fact that Windows can be configured differently on different computer systems.

Application Program Icon

Group Window

Group Icon (Minimized Group Window)

Figure 2.1 The opening screen of the Program Manager with Main window opened

The Program Manager window shown in Figure 2.1 contains five groups of programs labeled Main, Accessories, Games, Windows Applications, and Non-Windows Applications. The Main program group shown here has been opened and once opened is called a group window within the Program Manager window. The program groups are called **group windows** when opened because each group window organizes within itself a group of programs. For example, the Games group window organizes all the game programs into one group window. The other four program groups are shown in Figure 2.1 not as fully opened windows but as identical icons called **group icons**. The other four group icons are labeled: Accessories, Games, Windows Applications, and Non-Windows Applications. (When it is initially installed, Windows always includes the first three program groups; the other two are optional.) *Remember:* a group window can cover the entire screen, a portion of the screen or appear simply as a group icon. When you want to open a group window, you double-click on the group icon. For example, if you double-click on the Accessories group icon, the screen will then display the Accessories group window. Likewise, clicking on any other group icon in the Program Manager window will open another group window.

Now, let's make certain the definitions of icons and windows that you will need in order to proceed as you use Windows are understood:

Group icons. The program groups within the Program Manager that are reduced to identical symbols and may be located at the bottom of your window until each is opened.

Group window. An opened program group within the Program Manager window. (See the Main group window in Figure 2.1).

Application Program icon. A symbol that identifies an application program that exists within the group window but that has been minimized to an icon. These icons are also known as **program item icons**. The program item icons shown in Figure 2.1 are: File Manager, Control Panel, Print Manager, Clipboard, DOS prompt, and Windows Setup. When you double-click on a program item icon, it will start the application program and load its related documents.

Main Group Applications

Programs that help you manage the Windows environment are located in the Main group window.

Figure 2.2

File Manager icon

File Manager

File Manager. The File Manager application is used to help you manage your computer files. It permits you to find, move, copy, delete, rename, or print a file.

Figure 2.3

DOS Prompt icon

DOS Prompt

DOS Prompt. The DOS Prompt permits you to access DOS. To return to Windows, key "Exit" and press [Enter].

Figure 2.4

Print Manager icon

Print Manager

Print Manager. The Print Manager monitors the printing activity.

Figure 2.5
Control Panel icon

Control Panel

Control Panel. The Control Panel lets you adjust the appearance and performance of Windows. For example, it lets you adjust the spacing between items on your desktop and, if you have a color monitor, change the colors of the screen elements.

Figure 2.6
Clipboard icon

Clipboard

Clipboard. The Clipboard allows you to take text and graphics from one application and move it to another application.

Figure 2.7
Windows Setup icon

Windows Setup

Windows Setup. The Windows Setup program helps you install ("set up") new applications and change hardware configurations.

Accessories Group Applications

Very useful in doing routine work, Windows accessories include the following applications.

Figure 2.8
Write program icon

Write

Write. Write is an easy-to-use word processing program that permits you to key in, edit, save, and print documents.

Figure 2.9
Paintbrush program icon

Paintbrush

Paintbrush. Paintbrush is a drawing program that allows you to create color images that can be placed in documents and printed.

Figure 2.10
Calendar program icon

Calendar

Calendar. The Calendar program is a daily appointment book or monthly organizer with an alarm.

Figure 2.11
Clock icon

Clock

Clock. The time is found in the clock program, which provides a time display (analog or digital).

Figure 2.12
Cardfile icon

Cardfile

Cardfile. A cardfile provides an electronic "Rolodex®" file for storing, sorting, and selecting data.

Figure 2.13
Notepad icon

Notepad

Notepad. The notepad is a type of text-editor or mini-word processor for jotting down short notes and messages.

Figure 2.14
Calculator icon

Calculator

Calculator. An electronic calculator program provides the capability for doing a variety of mathematical calculations.

Games Group Applications

Solitaire and Reversi are included in the Games group.

Figure 2.15

Solitaire game icon

Solitaire

Solitaire. Solitaire is a computerized version of the popular card game.

Figure 2.16

Reversi game icon

Reversi

Reversi. Reversi is an electronic board game provided with Windows.

Non-Windows Applications

This group contains any application you may have installed on your computer system that is not specifically designed and provided with the Windows program. For instance, before beginning to use Windows you may have installed on your computer and been using *WordPerfect, Lotus 1-2-3,* or any one of dozens of popular application programs. With Windows, you may continue to use these popular programs. For example, to run your existing and installed WordPerfect program, you double-click on the Non-windows group icon. This action opens the group window and reveals the WordPerfect application. You then double-click on the WordPerfect application icon, which takes you to DOS and opens the WordPerfect application program. When you finish using the application, you exit WordPerfect and are automatically returned to Windows Program Manager. How many icons are in the Non-Windows application group? That depends on the number of programs you have installed.

Windows Applications

The Windows Applications group contains other applications designed to run under Windows. For example, *Microsoft Word for Windows* and *Microsoft Excel for Windows* will appear in this group window when it is opened, if they are installed on your computer. Here, too, the number of icons in the Windows Application program window depends on how many programs designed to run under Windows are installed on your system.

To see the program item icons and start the applications, you must open a group window by double-clicking on its icon. Once opened, the position of the window on the desktop and the window layout can be arranged to suit your taste.

EXERCISE 2 • 1 OPENING, ARRANGING, AND CLOSING GROUP WINDOWS

1. Start Windows if it is not already active.

2. Open the Accessories group window by double-clicking on the Accessories group icon at the bottom of the Program Manager window. You can see which applications are grouped under Accessories by looking at the program item icons in the Accessories window.

3. Open the Games group window by double-clicking on the Games group icon at the bottom of the Program Manager window. You now have two or three group windows opened, as shown in Figure 2.17.

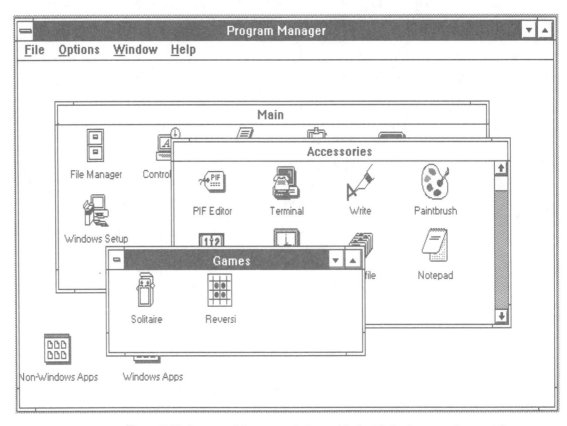

Figure 2.17 Program Manager window with the Main, Accessories, and Game windows opened

As you learned in Session 1, windows can be arranged in tile or cascade format by selecting the Window option on the Program Manager menu bar and then selecting Tile or Cascade.

4. Select the Cascade option from the Window menu. Figure 2.18 shows group windows displayed in cascade format. As you can see, the Cascade option layers group windows into a stack with titles showing; the active window is always in front of the stack, on the top layer.

5. Select the Tile option from the Window menu. As shown in Figure 2.19, the Tile option divides the Program Manager window evenly among the open group windows and shows the windows side by side, rather than overlapping.

6. Open the Windows Application group window by double-clicking on the Windows Application group icon at the bottom of the Program Manager window.

7. Select the Tile option from the Window menu. The open group windows are now evenly distributed in the Program Manager window.

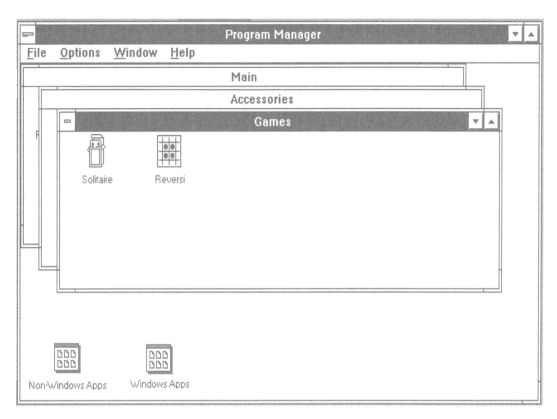

Figure 2.18 Program Manager window with the Main, Accessories, and Game windows arranged in cascade format

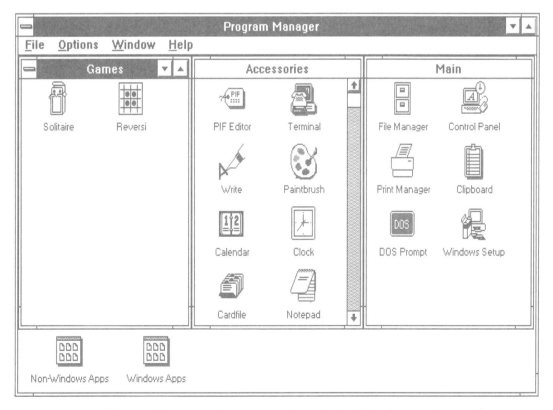

Figure 2.19 Program Manager window with the Main, Accessories, and Game windows arranged in tile format

8. Close the Games group window.

    a. Click on the Games window to select it.

    b. Double-click on the Control-menu box to close the Games window.

9. Close the Windows Application group window by double-clicking on its Control menu box. You now have two group windows open—Main and Accessories.

10. Move the windows so that they are placed in the locations as shown in Figure 2.20, if they do not already appear in that location.

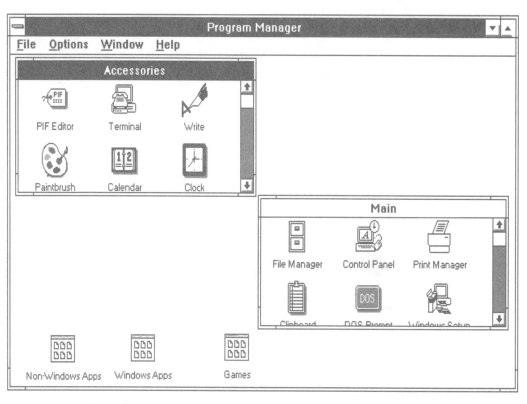

Figure 2.20 Program Manager with Accessories and Main groups

Modifying Group Windows

So far you have been working with group windows created when Windows was installed on your hard disk. Some day you will, no doubt, install new programs or add, remove, or change a group window. To do so, you can use either the Control Panel or the Program Manger. Later you will learn to use the Control Panel. For now let's use the Program Manager to modify the group windows.

    Resizing Group Windows. When you cascade or tile windows, the software determines the window size. (Whenever software makes a predetermined choice for you, that choice or setting is called the **default**). At times, however, you will want to control the size of your windows, that is change the default settings. You can resize windows to suit your needs by selecting and dragging one of the three types of window borders (horizontal, vertical, or corner). If you drag on a horizontal border, you will make the window taller or shorter. If you drag on a vertical border, you will make the window wider or narrower. If you drag from one of the corners, you can change two sides of the window with one movement.

EXERCISE 2 • 2 RESIZING A WINDOW

1. Position the pointer over the left-hand border of the Main group window. When the pointer is in the correct position, it will change to a double-headed arrow ($\Longleftrightarrow$).

2. Drag the border to the left until it is at the left margin of the Program Manager window.

3. Click on the Accessories group window to select it.

4. Position the pointer over the right-hand border of the Accessories group window, and drag the border to the right until it is at the right margin of the Program Manager window (Figure 2.21).

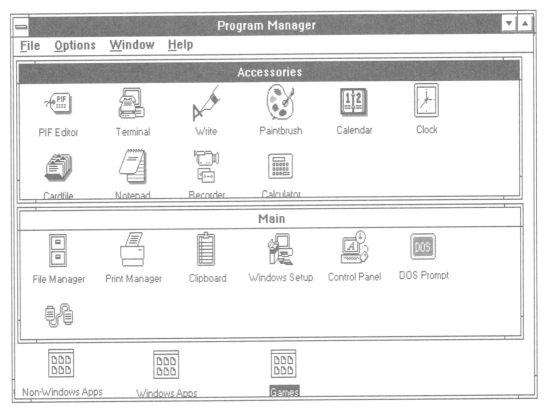

Figure 2.21 Main group window and Accessories group window rearranged one beneath the other

Minimizing, Maximizing, and Restoring Windows. As you have already seen, it is easy to size individual windows within the Program Manager. At times, however, you will want to temporarily enlarge an individual window to fill the entire screen. Three sizing functions are available from each window to help you quickly minimize, maximize, or restore a window:

● **Minimize.** Minimize reduces the active window to an icon, making it disappear from inside the Program Manager window and reappear at the bottom of the window as an icon. The window is still available and is not closed. Minimize allows more room on your desktop.

● **Maximize.** Maximize enlarges the active window to its maximum size so that it fills the entire window—helpful if you need a larger view of one window.

● **Restore.** When a window has been minimized or maximized, Restore returns the window to its original size.

If you are using a mouse, you can use the three sizing buttons located in the upper right-hand corner of the window (Figure 2-22). Clicking on a button activates it. For example, clicking on the Minimize button will minimize the window to an icon, and clicking on the Maximize button will enlarge the window to fill the entire desktop. Once you select the Maximize button, it is replaced by the Restore button, which appears below the title bar.

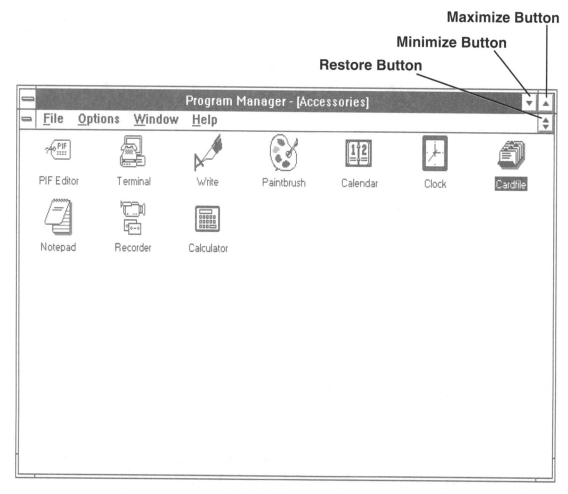

Figure 2.22 Upper right-hand corner of a window showing the Minimize, Maximize, and Restore buttons

EXERCISE 2 . 3   MINIMIZING, MAXIMIZING, AND RESTORING GROUP WINDOWS

Using the Sizing Buttons

1. Click on the Main window to select it.

2. Click on the Minimize button. The window will shrink to an icon at the bottom of the desktop.

3. Click on the Program Manager's maximize button. Notice that the maximized window has no borders and that it has a Restore button (on the menu bar) to restore the window to its original size and location.

4. Click on the Restore button on the menu bar. The Program Manager's window will be restored to its size and location before it was maximized.

Using the Control Menu

The minimize, maximize, and restore options on the Control menu can also be used to perform the same functions as the sizing buttons.

5. Click on the Games group window icon to display the Control menu.

6. Select the Maximize option. Notice that the window fills the entire screen and covers up the other open windows.

7. Click on the Restore button. The Games window is restored to an open window in the Program Manager.

8. Click once on the Control-menu box of the Games group window to display the Control menu.

9. Select the Close option.

Rearranging the Program Item Icons. The Program Manager includes an option on two drop down menus, the Options menu and the Window menu, to assist you in arranging the Program icons. As you resize windows, using a mouse to rearrange them and working with program icons, your active window can become disorganized. The Arrange Icons option on the Window menu organizes all the program icons in the active window and "squares up" all the icons, saving you the time and trouble.

It is important to have the Auto Arrange option on the Options menu active when resizing windows. This option automatically rearranges the icons in the window to fit the new window's size. In this way, this option helps you determine how large the window needs to be during resizing. Of course, you can make a window any size you want. If the icons do not fit, a scroll bar appears at the bottom or side of the window so you can view icons not visible in the window.

EXERCISE 2 . 4   ARRANGING WINDOWS AND GROUP ICONS

Setting the Auto Arrange Option

The Auto Arrange option on the Options menu is active (selected) when a check mark appears before the option on the menu (Figure 2-23).

The Auto Arrange option, like many of the Options menu items, can be toggled on and off. If the option is active (checked), it is toggled on; selecting it again will toggle it off, making it inactive. If the option is inactive (not checked) selecting it will make it active. Let's practice using the Auto Arrange option.

Figure 2.23

The Auto Arrange option on the Options menu

Options
√ Auto Arrange
Minimize on Use

1. Point on the Options menu to display the menu.

2. Verify that the Auto Arrange option is active (checked). If it is active, close the menu by clicking on the desktop—not the menu. If it is inactive (not checked), click on the Auto Arrange option to make it active.

3. Click on the Maximize button of the Accessories group window.

4. Drag the program icons so they are randomly placed around the screen.

5. Select the Arrange Icons option on the Window menu. The icons will jump into an orderly line.

Using the Auto Arrange Option

6. Click on the Auto Arrange option on the Options menu to deselect it (remove the check mark).

7. Drag the program item icons in the window so that they are arranged in two columns of five icons each down the left side of the screen.

8. Click on the Restore button on the menu bar. Notice that the icons remain in two columns. Since you cannot see all ten icons, scroll bars are displayed at the right side of the window.

9. Select the Auto Arrange option from the Options menu.

10. Maximize the Accessories window. Notice that the icons are automatically arranged across the top of the window.

11. Click on the Restore button. Notice the icons are again arranged across the window. Since all the icons are in view, scroll bars are not displayed.

VIEW 2
WORKING WITH GROUPS

PREVIEW

As you have seen, at times the active window covers up some or all of the other group windows, making it difficult to access the other windows. To eliminate this problem, the Window menu lists all the groups that have been created, thereby letting you quickly switch between groups. A check mark will be placed on the menu next to a window's name when it has been activated (see Figure 2.24). To make a another group active, just click on its name on the menu. If the chosen window is minimized, it will also be opened. If the layout of the windows is in a cascade format, the window selected will be brought to the front of the stack of windows.

Window	
Cascade	Shift+F5
Tile	Shift+F4
Arrange Icons	
1 Windows Apps	
2 Aldus	
3 Non-Windows Apps	
4 Word Processing	
5 Games	
√ 6 Accessories	
7 Main	

EXERCISE 2 • 5   SWITCHING BETWEEN GROUPS

1. Select the Games group from the Window menu. The Games group window is opened and displayed as an active window.

2. Select the Main group from the Window menu. The Main group window is opened over the other windows.

3. Select the Tile option from the Window menu.

4. Minimize the Games group window by clicking on the Minimize button.

5. Select the Tile option from the Window menu to rearrange the open windows.

Creating Group Windows

In Windows, you have the ability to customize your groups and the programs within the groups to fit your special needs. One way to customize Windows is to add or create a new group or a new program item. The process for both adding a new group and a new program item is similar, but we will look at each one separately. First, let's look at adding or creating a new group.

Creating a new group window will place a new, empty group in the Program Manager window. For example, you could create a new group window named "Word Processing" and place related items in it.

EXERCISE 2 • 6   CREATING A NEW GROUP WINDOW

1. Select New ... from the File menu. The New Program Object dialog box will appear, as shown in Figure 2.25.

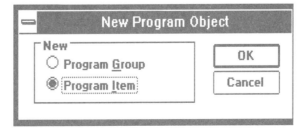

2. Click on the Program group option button.

3. Click on the OK button. The Program Group Properties dialog box will be displayed, as shown in Figure 2.26.

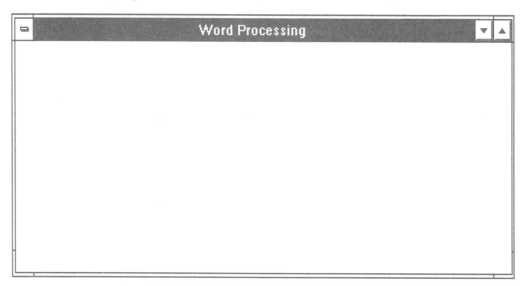

Figure 2.26

Program Group Properties dialog box

4. Key *Word Processing* in the Description text box to name the new group window. You do not need to fill in the Group File text box— the purpose of this box will be explained later.

5. Click on the OK button. The new program group will be added and displayed as the active window, as shown in Figure 2.27. Notice that the title on the title bar is the same as the description you keyed in the Description text box.

Figure 2.27 Word Processing group window

Adding Program Items to a Group Window

You can add program items to a group window in three different ways:

- By copying a program item icon from one group to another
- By moving a program item icon from one group to another
- By adding a new program item icon to a group

Copying a Program Item Between Groups

The two ways to copy a program item between groups are: (1) use the Copy option available on the Windows menu, and (2) use the mouse to drag a program icon from one group window to another, a process that actually copies the icon.

EXERCISE 2 • 7   COPYING A PROGRAM ITEM ICON BETWEEN GROUPS

Using the Mouse

1. Select the Tile option on the Window menu to display the three open windows.

2. Press and hold **[Ctrl]**.

3. Place the mouse pointer on the Write program icon in the Accessories group window and press the mouse button.

4. Drag the Write program icon to the Word Processing group window and release the mouse button and **[Ctrl]**. The Write program icon now appears in both the Accessories group window and the Word Processing group window. The Write program can be accessed from either group (Figure 2.28).

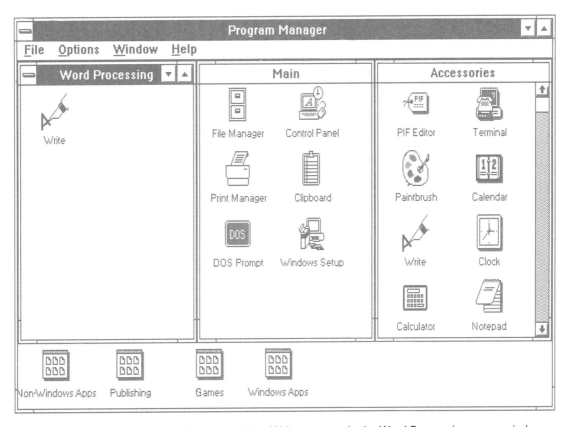

Figure 2.28 Screen with the Write program in the Word Processing group window and in the Accessories group window

Using the Copy Option

5. Click on the Notepad program icon in the Accessories group window to select it. (You may have to use the scroll bar to bring it into view.)

6. Select the Copy option from the File menu (**[Alt]** + **[F]** then **[C]**). The Copy Program Item dialog box with a drop-down box inside it will be displayed (Figure 2.29).

Figure 2.29

Copy Program Item dialog box

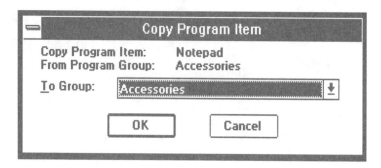

7. Display the list box by pressing **[Alt]** and the **[Down Arrow]**.

8. Select the Word Processing group window by pressing the **[Down Arrow]** until the Word Processing group name is highlighted.

9. Press **[Enter]** to select the word processing window. As before, the selected program is copied to the Word Processing group window.

Moving a Program Item Between Groups

In Session 1, you learned to move an icon by dragging it to a new location. When a program item icon is dragged from one group window to another, it is moved, not copied. That means that the program item icon will appear only in the new location.

EXERCISE 2 • 8   MOVING A PROGRAM ITEM BETWEEN GROUPS

Using the Mouse

1. Point on the Notepad icon in the Word Processing group window and drag the icon to the Main group window. Notice that the Notepad icon is "removed" from the Word Processing window and placed in the Main group window.

Using the Move Option

2. Select the Notepad icon in the Main group window.

3. Select the Move option from the File menu (**[Alt] [F]** + **[M]**).

4. Display the list box by pressing **[Alt]** and the **[Down Arrow]**.

5. Select the Word Processing group name by pressing the **[Down Arrow]** until the Word Processing group name is highlighted.

6. Press **[Enter]**.

Adding a Program Item to a Group Window

If you want to add a new program item to the Program Manager, you can create a new item if you know: (1) the directory in which the new program has been installed and (2) the command needed to run the application. For example, let's assume you want to install a new word processing program called "Micro Writer" in the Windows directory on your hard disk, and the command needed to run the new program is WRITE.EXE.

Knowing this information, you select the New... command from the File menu and click on the Program Item option button. In the Program Item Properties dialog box, you enter the description of the new item, and in the Command Line text box, you enter the command needed to run the application. In our example, you know the command is WRITE.EXE, but if you cannot remember (or do not know) exactly where it is located on your hard disk, you can click on the Browse... command button to display the Browse dialog box.

The Browse dialog box contains a listing of files and directories that you can scroll through until you locate the command. When you select the appropriate command, it will be placed in the appropriate text box. Clicking on the OK command button will return you to the Program Item Properties dialog box, and clicking on the OK command button again will record your selections and create the new program item.

EXERCISE 2 • 9 ADDING A NEW APPLICATION TO A GROUP WINDOW

1. Select the Word Processing group window.

2. Select the New... option from the File menu.

3. Verify that the Program Item option button is selected; then click on the OK command button.

4. Key the program name *Micro Writer* in the Description text box.

5. Click on the Browse... Option Button to display the Browse dialog box.

6. Verify that the directory containing the Windows program is selected. In our example, this is the Windows directory, as shown in Figure 2.30.

Figure 2.30

Browse dialog box with Files and Directories listings

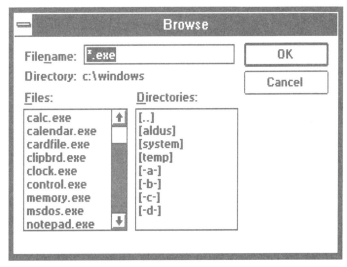

7. Select the write.exe file from the "Files:" listing box. You will need to scroll to locate the file at the bottom of the list. Notice that the filename write.exe is transferred to the "Filename" text box (Figure 2.31).

Figure 2.31

Browse dialog box with Filename
text box completed

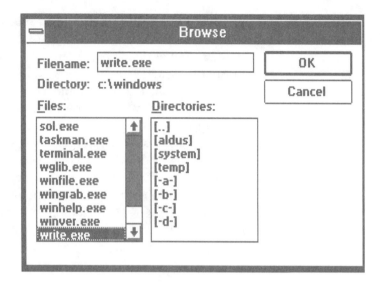

8. Click on the OK command button

9. Verify that the Program Item Properties dialog box contains the text lines shown in Figure 2.32.

Figure 2.32

Completed Program Item Properties
dialog box

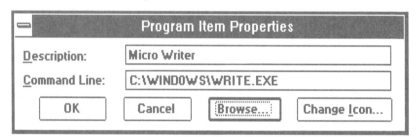

10. Click on the OK command button. The new program item icon "Micro Writer" should be displayed in the Word Processing group window.

Changing the Properties of Groups and Program Items

Another way to customize the Program Manager is to change an item's icon or change the title of a group or item. This is called changing a group or item's properties. Changing properties is appropriate when you find a group's title is not descriptive enough or an item's icon is not representative enough.

EXERCISE 2 • 10 CHANGING GROUP PROPERTIES

1. Minimize the Word Processing group window to an icon.

2. Click on the Word Processing group icon to display the Control menu.

3. Select the Properties... option from the File menu. The Program Group Properties dialogue box will be displayed (Figure 2.33). You change the group name by keying in the new name in the Description text box.

4. Key the new name *Publishing* and click on the OK command button. Notice that the group icon has been renamed.

Figure 2.33

Program Group Properties dialog box

Program Group Properties

Description: Word Processing

Group File: C:\WINDOWS\WORDPROC.GRP

[OK] [Cancel]

Just as you can change the properties of a group, you can change the properties of a program item. Rather than selecting the "Group," bring up the Select Icon dialogue box, which allows you to change the icon for the item.

The Select Icon dialogue box displays the current icon selected for the item and has a View Next button. Choosing the View Next button cycles through the available choices of icons. After you choose OK in the Program Item Properties dialogue box, the new icon and any other changes you made will take effect.

For the next exercise, let's pretend that the Control Panel program is actually a desktop publishing program. We will copy it to our publishing group and change its properties—its name and icon.

EXERCISE 2 • 11 CHANGING PROGRAM ITEM PROPERTIES

1. Open the Publishing group window by double clicking on the Publishing group icon.

2. Copy the Control Panel icon from the Main group to the Publishing Group. (Remember to press and hold down **[Ctrl]** while you drag the icon.)

3. Verify that the Control Panel program is selected in the Publishing group.

4. Select the Properties option from the File menu. The Program Item Properties dialog box is displayed, as shown in Figure 2.34.

Figure 2.34

Program Item Properties dialog box

Program Item Properties

Description: Control Panel

Command Line: CONTROL.EXE

[OK] [Cancel] [Browse...] [Change Icon...]

5. Key the new description *Easy Publisher* in the Description text box.

6. Click on the Change Icon... command button.

7. Click on the View Next command button until the icon that consists of three "A's" is displayed, as shown in Figure 2.35.

Figure 2.35

Select Icon dialog box

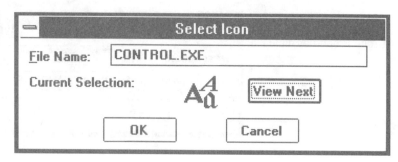

8. Click on the OK command button to select the new icon.

9. Click on the OK command button on the Program Item Properties dialog box. The Item Properties are now displayed in the Publishing group window.

Deleting a Group Window or a Program Item from a Group

When you delete a program or a group of programs from your system, you should also delete the program icon. When you delete a group window, you also delete all the program icons within that group.

EXERCISE 2 • 12   DELETING A PROGRAM ITEM AND A GROUP

Deleting a Program Item

1. Select the Easy Publisher icon in the Publishing group window.

2. Select the Delete option from the File menu (**[Delete]**). The Delete message box will be displayed. Clicking on the Yes command button will activate the command; clicking on the No command button will cancel the command.

3. Click on the Yes command button. The program item Easy Publisher will be removed from the Publishing group window.

Deleting a Group

4. Reduce the Publishing group to an icon.

5. Select the Publishing group by clicking on its icon.

6. Select the Delete option from the File menu (**[Delete]**). The Delete message box will be displayed.

7. Click on the Yes command button to delete the group. As shown in Figure 2.36, the Publishing group has been deleted.

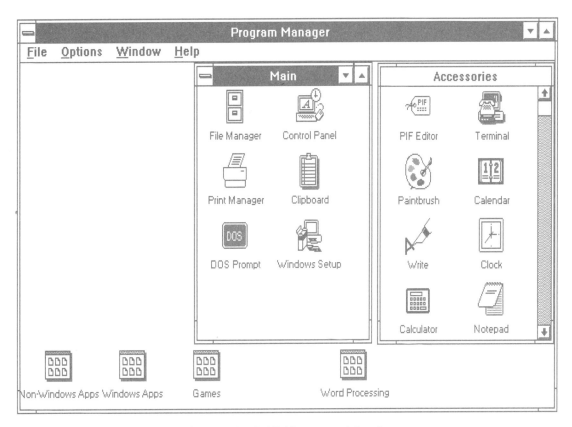

Figure 2.36 Screen with Publishing group deleted

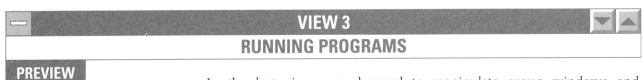

VIEW 3
RUNNING PROGRAMS

PREVIEW

In the last view, you learned to manipulate group windows and application icons. In this view, you will learn how to use these windows and icons to start or "run" your application programs.

There are two ways you can start an application—directly and indirectly. An application is started directly by double-clicking on the application icon or by keying in the WIN command followed by the application name when you start Windows from the DOS prompt. An application is started indirectly by using the Run... command on the File menu.

EXERCISE 2 ● 13   STARTING AN APPLICATION DIRECTLY

Starting an Application from the DOS Prompt.

1. Exit Windows and return to the system DOS prompt (usually C:>). When the Exit Windows message box is displayed, verify that Save Changes is unchecked; then click on the OK command button.

2. Key the command *WIN*, space once, key the application name *Write*, and press **[Enter]**. Your command should look like this: C:>WIN WRITE **[Enter]**.

You will see the Write application program, as shown in Figure 2.37. You will learn to use this application in a later view. For now, you will just close the application (instructions for closing the application are provided in Step 3).

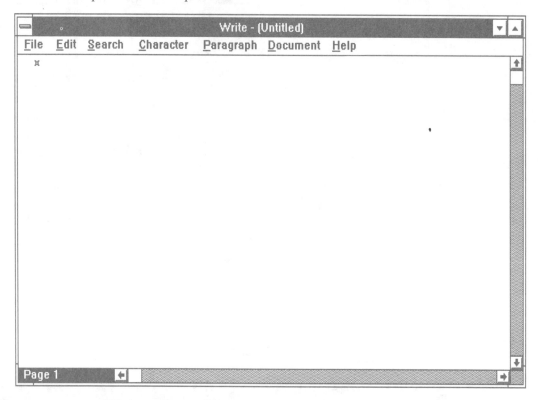

Figure 2.37 Windows Write application program opening screen

3. Select the Exit command from the File menu. You should always select the Exit command because Exit will prompt you about saving your work (if you have started a document) before you issue the close command. Once the application is closed, you will be returned to the Program Manager.

4. Double-click on the Program Manager icon to open it, if it is not opened.

5. Double-click on the Accessories group icon to open the Accessories group window.

Starting an Application from the Program Manager

6. Double click on the Write program icon in the Accessories window. The application will begin as before.

7. Select the Exit command from the File menu. The application will be closed, and you will be returned to the Program Manager.

Using the Run... Command

You can start any application from the Program Manager, whether it has an icon or not. The Run... command on the File menu allows you to start an application by giving the Program Manager the details it needs to execute the command. For example, if you want to use a program you don't work with very often, a program you didn't bother adding to a group window, you can start it by selecting the Run... command, which brings up the Run dialog box, shown in Figure 2.38.

Figure 2.38

Run dialog box

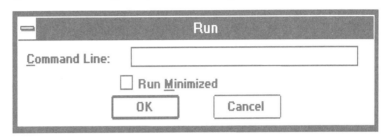

When you use the Run... command, you need to know where the application is stored on the hard disk (the path) and the command that starts the application. For example, if you have installed the Write program in the C:\WINDOWS directory and the command that starts the application is WRITE.EXE, you would key *C:\WINDOWS\WRITE.EXE* in the Command Line text box. When you exit the application, you will be returned to the Program Manager.

EXERCISE 2 • 14   USING THE RUN... COMMAND

Opening an Application and Exiting Windows

1. Select the Run... command from the File menu.

2. Key the command *C:\WINDOWS\WRITE.EXE* (or key the correct path for your system) in the Command Line text box and press **[Enter]**. Again, the Write program is opened.

3. Select the Exit command from the File menu. The application will be closed, and you will be returned to the Program Manager.

4. Double-click on the Program Manager's Control-menu box to exit Windows. When the Exit Windows messages box is displayed, verify that Save Changes is unchecked, and then click on the OK Command button.

SUMMARY

In this Session you learned the purpose and function of the Program Manager and about several programs in the Main group window that help you manage the Windows environment. You practiced organizing group windows and application program icons. You also customized the Program Manager by copying, moving, and adding program icons and group windows. You learned about one of the strengths of the Windows program when you switched between groups and created a new group window.

The ability to minimize, maximize, and restore group windows became clearer while doing the exercises in Session 2, as did arranging windows and group items, deleting program items and a group, and, of course, starting and quitting an application and exiting Windows.

• • • • • • • • • • • • •

OBJECTIVES

When you complete this session, you will be able to:

- Start File Manager, explain its purpose and function, and exit File Manager.

- Expand and collapse the Directory Tree.

- Open and close a directory window.

- Format and label disks.

SESSION 3

FILE MANAGER PART I

VIEWS
Understanding the File Manager
Working with Disks and Disk Drives

FILE MANAGER - PART I

PREVIEW

In order to understand the File Manager, you must understand something about computer memory and storage. Your computer manipulates and processes data in electronic memory called **RAM** (**R**andom **A**ccess **M**emory). The application programs and contents of the documents you use in Windows reside in RAM when they are active. When you exit a program, turn your computer off, or lose power to your computer, the content of RAM is erased.

The two drawbacks of electronic memory are (1) it is limited in size and (2) it is erased when the power is turned off. For these reasons, magnetic storage is used to save application programs and data documents for extended periods or when the computer is not operating. Magnetic storage may be in the form of a hard disk inside your computer or an external floppy disk.

Think of a disk as a kind of electronic file cabinet. The files in this electronic file cabinet are the program instructions or data documents saved on the disk. Thus, computer files are categorized as program files or data files. While file cabinets have drawers and folders to help organize their contents, computer disks rely on directories and subdirectories to organize their magnetic files.

The File Manager is designed to help you find, view, manage, and use your files easily and efficiently. That's why the File Manager icon is a file cabinet (Figure 3.1). With the File Manager you are able to get a graphic view of your disk's contents. It shows you all the directories and how they relate to each other in a window called Directory Tree. In addition, you can view the contents of multiple directories at the same time. You can even change the type and amount of directory information that is displayed.

Figure 3.1

File Manager icon

File Manager

Starting File Manager

When Windows was installed on your system, File Manager was installed in the Main program group. Follow the steps in Exercise 3.1 to start the File Manager now so that you can see the graphical display it presents you.

EXERCISE 3 • 1 STARTING FILE MANAGER

1. Start Windows if it is not currently running.

2. Double-click on the Main window to activate it.

3. Double-click on the File Manager icon. As illustrated in Figure 3.2, the File Manager now displays two open windows—the File Manager window and a Directory Tree window. Your Directory Tree display will show items different from those illustrated in Figure 3.2, but the basic window is the same.

File Manager Menu Bar

Directory Tree
Window

File Manager
Status Bar

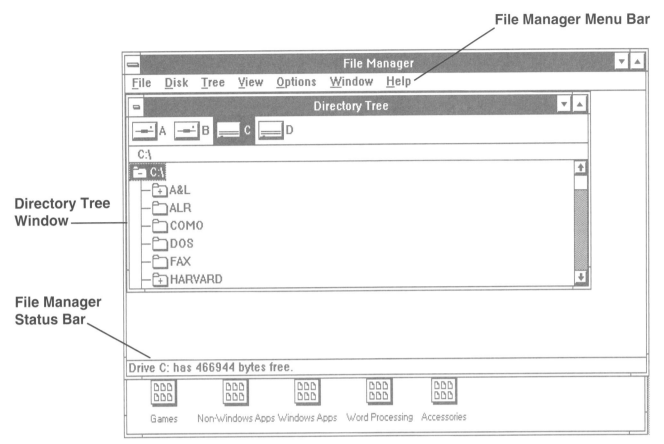

Figure 3.2 File Manager window with Directory Tree window open

4. Click on the Maximize button to enlarge the Directory Tree window. Note that the title bar changes to reflect the new combination: it displays "File Manager-[Directory Tree]," as illustrated in Figure 3.3. Again, your screen will show some different items, but the basic window is the same.

Understanding the Elements in the File Manager Window

The File Manager offers convenient ways to manage your files and directories, but to take advantage of its power and use the File Manager effectively, you must be familiar with the elements in the File Manager window display. First, as you can see in Figure 3.3, the File Manager menu bar remains on the screen for you to access.

Now let's review the other elements in the window display.

Disk drives. Below the File Manager menu bar are the disk drive icons, which identify by letter and type the disk drives that you can access. This display will vary from one computer system to another. The icons simulate the look of floppy disk drives and hard disk drives. To change the active (highlighted) drive, click on another drive icon.

Directory path. Below the drive icons you will see the directory path (for example, C:\ or A:\ or B:\), which shows the course or roadway to the current directory. See Figure 3.4 for a full explanation of the directory path.

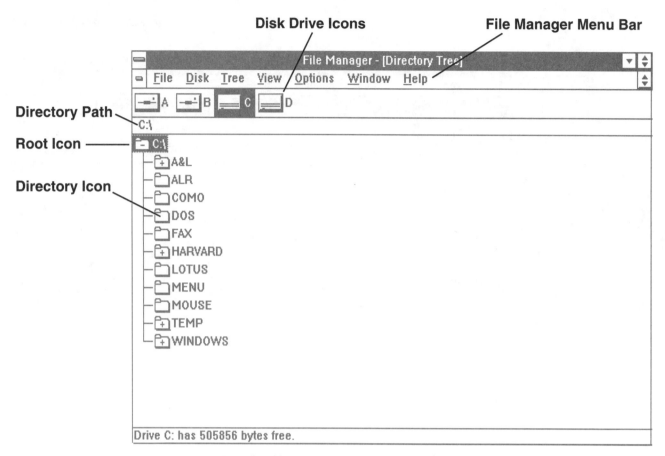

Figure 3.3 Maximized Directory Tree window

Directory Path

The directory path shows the course or roadway to the current directory. For most systems, the directory path will display "C:\" only, which represents the root directory. But your display may show something else.

In path notations such as "C:\," the backward slash (\) is used to separate directories and subdirectories. For example, the path directory "C:\WP\MSWORD\WORD5" indicates that the "WORD5" subdirectory is located in the "MSWORD" subdirectory which is in the "WP" directory on the "C" drive. Note that you read the path backwards, following the backward slashes all the way to the root directory.

Figure 3.4 Explanation of Directory Path

Directory icon. Each directory in the tree is identified by a file folder icon, and the highlighted directory is the active one. Think of the Directory Tree as an upside-down tree; its main root (C:\) is at the top and its major branches (directories) and lesser branches (subdirectories) flow downward toward the bottom. Directory icons will be covered more fully later in this view.

Status Bar. At the bottom of the screen is the status bar, which tells you how much free space is available on the current disk.

Expanding the Directory Tree

Directories and subdirectories will be discussed in detail in Session 4. For now, think of a directory as a group of files and a subdirectory as a subgroup of files. How can you tell whether a directory has a subdirectory? Look for a plus sign (+) in a directory icon; the plus sign tells you that a directory does have subdirectories.

To view and work with directories, you can expand them one at a time by clicking on any directory icon with a plus sign. Or you can expand the entire Directory Tree by selecting the Expand All option from the Tree menu. An expanded Directory Tree will appear, similar to the one shown in Figure 3.5.

Expanded Directory

Expanded Directory Tree

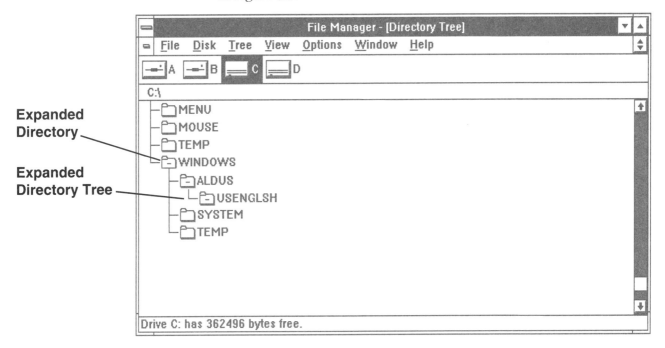

Figure 3.5 Expanded Directory Tree window

The exercises in this session assume that Windows has been installed in a Windows subdirectory on drive C. If this is different for your system, your instructor will give you alternate instructions.

EXERCISE 3 • 2   EXPANDING THE DIRECTORY TREE

1. Find the WINDOWS directory, and note that its file folder shows a plus sign (+). Click once—only once, or you will open the directory itself—on the WINDOWS directory icon. The Directory Tree will expand the display, showing the subdirectories two levels below WINDOWS. In Figure 3.5, note that none of the subdirectory icons displays a plus sign, so you know that there are no more subdirectories below this level.

2. Select the Expand All option from the Tree menu. The Directory Tree will display the root and all its directories and subdirectories similar to

the display in Figure 3.5. Scroll bars will be displayed if the Directory Tree is too large to display in the Directory Tree window.

3. If necessary, scroll the Directory Tree using the scroll bar; then return to the root of the active drive by clicking on the up button at the top of the scroll box until the root (that is, C:\) is displayed.

Collapsing the Directory Tree

Once expanded, file folders that had a plus sign now display a minus (-) sign. When you click on a directory icon with a minus sign, the Directory Tree display collapses one level, and the plus sign replaces the minus. If you want to collapse all subdirectories, click on the root icon at the top of the directory window. All directories will disappear. The opposite is also true: when directories are collapsed, clicking on the root icon will expand the directory.

EXERCISE 3 . 3   COLLAPSING THE DIRECTORY TREE

1. Click on the Windows icon (it should currently display a minus sign). The subdirectories will collapse.

2. Scroll to the top of the Directory Tree window to display the C:\ root icon (Figure 3.6).

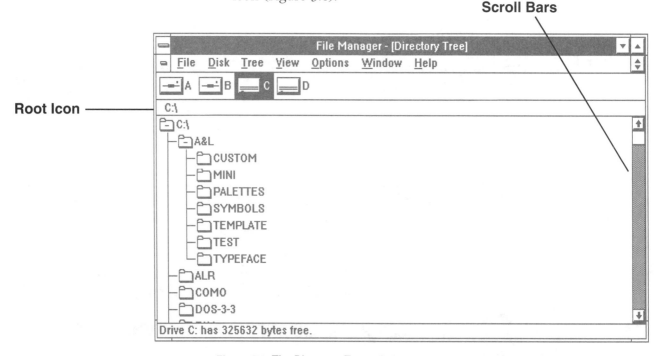

Figure 3.6 The Directory Tree window root icon

3. Click on the Directory Tree window root icon. All directories will disappear. Do not click on the root icon again; doing so will expand the directory.

Opening Directory Windows

As you have seen, the Directory Tree window shows the overall structure of a *disk's* contents, not a *directory's* contents. To display all the files in a directory, you need to see a **directory window**, such as the one shown in Figure 3.7.

To open a directory window, double-click on a directory icon. For example, to open the Excel directory window, double-click on the Excel directory icon. As in Figure 3.7, you will see a title bar at the top of the Directory Tree window that shows the directory path for EXCEL. At the bottom of the window, the status bar shows the total size (in bytes) of the selected (highlighted) file. It also shows the number of files in the directory. As you will learn later, you can keep more than one directory window open—a very convenient way to copy or move files from one directory to another.

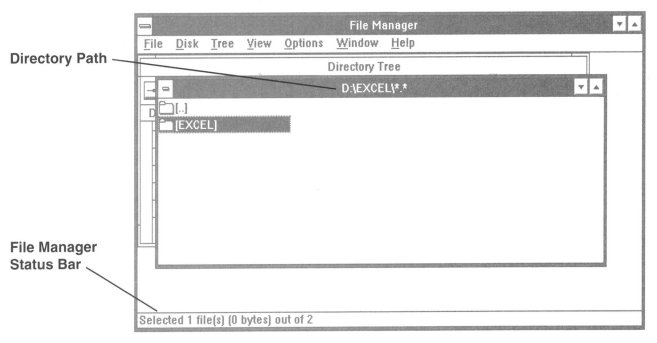

Figure 3.7 An active directory window

Identifying Icons in a Directory Window

In a directory window, four kinds of icons distinguish among the different directories and files:

Figure 3.8

Directory icon

Directory icon. A directory icon identifies each directory in the window. The directory names are listed in alphabetic order in brackets to distinguish them from files (for example, [SYSTEM]). The first directory icon is followed by [..], which represents the parent directory, the one above WINDOWS. The parent is the root C:\. Double-clicking on [..] will open the parent directory window.

Figure 3.9

Program file icon

Program file icon. In order to run application programs, you must double-click on the program file icon. These files always have the file extension .EXE, .COM, .PIF, or .BAT.

Figure 3.10

Document file icon

Document file icon. Document file icons represent data files created with a specific application program. For example, a document file icon with the label LETTER1.WRI represents a document created with the Windows Write program (Write attaches the .WRI file extension to its files).

Figure 3.11

Data file icon

Data file icon. All other files are represented by the data file icon. Data files are often used to support program files.

EXERCISE 3 . 4   OPENING AND CLOSING DIRECTORY WINDOWS

Opening a Directory Window

1. Expand the Directory Tree; then scroll to the Windows directory icon.

2. Double-click on the Windows directory icon to open the directory window.

3. Double-click on the System directory icon in the Windows directory window. A second directory window opens, and the status line changes to display the appropriate information about the active window.

4. Click on the Windows directory window (C:\WINDOWS) to select it. It is located behind the System directory window.

5. Double-click on the Temp directory icon in the Windows directory window. A third directory window now opens.

Closing a Directory Window

6. Double-click on the Temp directory window's control-menu box to close the directory window.

To close all the open directory windows, use the Close All Directories option on the Window menu.

7. Select the Close All Directories option from the Window menu. The two remaining windows close and the Directory Tree window opens.

Exiting File Manager

The best way to close File Manager is to select the Exit option on the File menu. A message box (see Figure 3.12) will appear asking you to confirm

Figure 3.12

Exit File Manager dialog box

that you really want to quit. Do ***not*** click on Save Settings. Reason: If changes you made to the File Manager menu options are saved, they will then become the new settings for presenting directory information. Although it is sometimes desirable to save your settings, doing so at this point can cause confusion.

EXERCISE 3 • 5   EXITING FILE MANAGER

1. Select the Exit Option from the File menu.

2. Verify that an X does not appear in the Save Settings check box. If there is an X, click on it to deselect the option.

3. Click on the OK command button to exit File Manager.

VIEW 2
WORKING WITH DISKS AND DISK DRIVES

PREVIEW

Like paper files, data files tend to accumulate. Again like paper files, disorganized data files are hard to find and frequently lost. In Windows, the process of saving a data file (it may be a word processing document, a spreadsheet, or data generated by any other application program) is easy enough: You use the File options Save or Save As.... But where you save your files and how you organize them will determine how easily you can find them when you want them. You must maintain files or they will get out of control.

To maintain files, you must know about hard disks and floppy disks. You can save files on your hard disk, but even a spacious hard disk can quickly become filled. On the other hand, floppy diskettes (or simply *disks*) are easy to use and portable; they can be carried to other machines. In this view, you will learn to prepare floppy disks to save files, that is, you will learn to format floppy disks.

Choosing Floppy Disks

What kind of disk should you use with your computer? The answer depends on what kind of disk drive or drives your system has.

Floppy disk drives come in two commonly-used sizes, 5¼ inch and 3½ inch. Your computer may have one floppy drive, or it may have one of each. Check it now.

How much data can a disk store? That depends on the disk *and* the disk drive in which it was formatted. Disk drives, as well as disks, are of two types: high-density (also called "high-capacity") or double-density (also called "low density"). The "density" determines the maximum amount of data that a disk can store. High-density disks will store approximately twice as much data as double-density disks.

Unfortunately, you cannot mix and match disks and drives randomly. Let's just say that you should match disks and disk drives not only by size but also by density: Use a high-density disk in a high-density drive and a double-density disk in a double-density drive. Now, that's easy enough, right? (Actually, you *can* use a double-density disk in a high-density drive but not vice versa. You will master the differences with some experience.)

In the exercises below you will format a high-density (or high-capacity) disk.

Formatting Floppy Disks

Before you can use a new floppy disk, it must be **formatted**. Formatting prepares a disk for use on a specific type of drive. The process imprints a disk with the information it needs to work in that particular kind of drive. The formatting process also erases all the information on a disk and is therefore potentially dangerous. As you will see in the exercise below, dialog boxes will protect you from erasing data accidentally. Dialog boxes will also ask you for information about your disk drive or diskette.

EXERCISE 3 • 6   FORMATTING A DISK

1. Use a felt pen to label a high-density disk *Quick Start*. Figure 3.13 shows you where to place the label on both 3½- and 5¼-inch disks.

Figure 3.13

Label placement on a 3½" disk and a 5¼" diskette

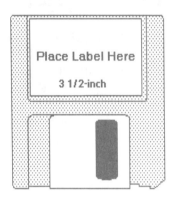
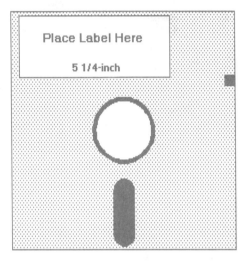

2. Start the File Manager if it is not already running.

3. Select the Format Diskette option from the Disk menu.

4. a. If you have only one floppy disk drive, the Format Diskette dialog box shown in Figure 3.14 will appear, warning you that all data will

Figure 3.14

Format Diskette warning box

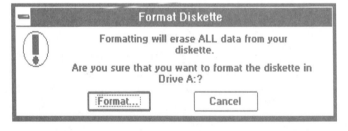

be erased from the disk when it is formatted. Click on the Format... command button to begin formatting; if you do not wish to format your disk, click on the Cancel command button.

b. If you have more than one floppy disk drive, a dialog box will appear (see Figure 3.15) asking you to select the drive that contains

Figure 3.15

Format Diskette select diskette dialog box

the disk to be formatted. Change the drive if necessary; then click on the OK command button. Next you will see the same warning (shown in Figure 3.14) that all data will be erased from the disk when it is formatted.

Click on the Format... command button to begin formatting; if you do not wish to format your disk, click on the Cancel command button.

5. The Format Diskette dialog box will change to display a message (Figure 3.16) asking you to insert your disk and indicate its capacity.

Figure 3.16

Format Diskette options dialog box

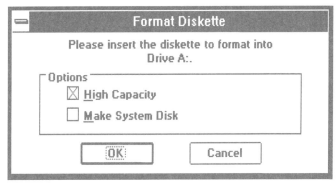

If you are using a high-density disk, check the High Capacity box; if not, leave this box blank. This dialog box also lets you create a system disk that can be used to boot or start your computer (you will not need to create a system disk in *Quick Start*).

6. Insert your *Quick Start* disk in the correct disk drive label-side up, with the oblong read/write slot facing the drive. *Hint:* Hold the disk in your right hand with your thumb on the label.

7. If you are using a high-density disk, verify that the High Capacity check box is selected; then click on the OK command button. You can cancel the format operation at any time by clicking on the Cancel button.

When formatting is complete, the status line displays the Format Complete message box shown in Figure 3.17. It also asks if you want to format another diskette.

8. Click on the No command button to end formatting.

Figure 3.17

Format Complete message box

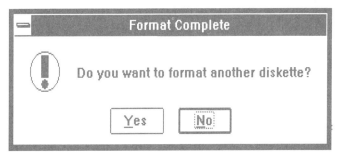

Accessing Disk Drives

All disk operations except formatting require that you first select the drive you want to use. Floppy disk drives are generally drive A and drive B (if the system has a second floppy drive); hard drives are designated drive C, D, E, and so on. Each disk drive available on your computer is represented by an icon on the directory window's drive icon bar.

You can select a drive by clicking on an icon on the disk drive icon bar in the Directory Tree window (See Figure 3.18). You can issue commands by selecting options from the File Manager menu bar.

**Disk Drive
Icon Bar**

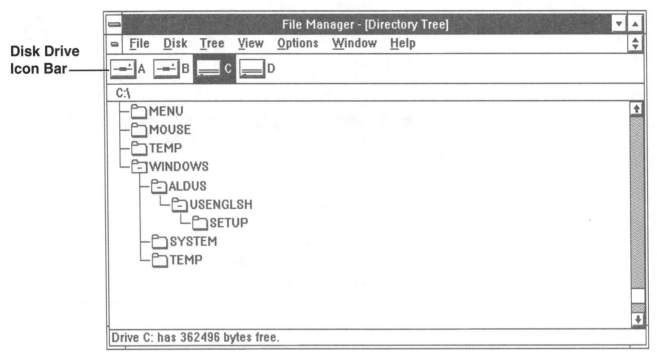

Figure 3.18 Disk drive icon bar

EXERCISE 3 ● 7   SELECTING A DISK DRIVE

1. Select the drive that contains your newly formatted *Quick Start* disk.
The disk drive icon for that drive becomes highlighted.

If you select a drive without a disk in it, a System Error message box
will tell you that the drive is not ready (Figure 3.19). Insert the disk in
that drive, close the
drive gate, and click
on the Retry com-
mand button. If you
do not wish to access
the drive, click on
the Cancel command
button.

Figure 3.19

System error message box

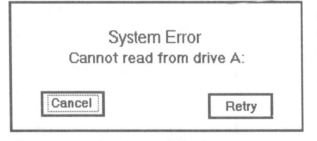

2. Select drive C; then remove your *Quick Start* disk from the drive.

3. Select the drive that contained your *Quick Start* disk. Wait until the
System Error message box is displayed.

4. Reinsert your *Quick Start* disk into the same drive.

5. Click on the Retry command button to select the drive once again.

Labeling Disks

Just as a paper label identifies a disk on the outside, a disk label identifies
a disk on the inside, that is, electronically, with a magnetic label. The label
is displayed on the Directory Tree window just below the drive icon bar
as shown in Figure 3.20.

Figure 3.20

Directory Tree window showing disk label

Volume Label

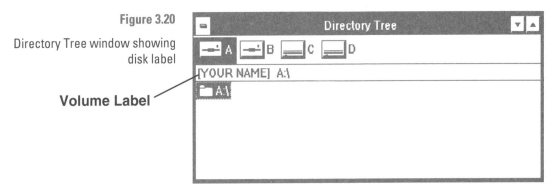

EXERCISE 3 . 8   LABELING A DISK

1. Verify that your *Quick Start* disk is in one of the floppy drives. Then select that drive.

2. Select the Label Disk option from the Disk menu. The Label Disk dialog box, shown in Figure 3.21, will be displayed with the cursor already in the Label text box.

Figure 3.21

Label Disk dialog box

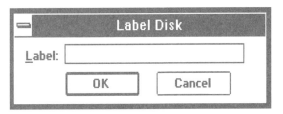

3. Key your last name. If your last name is longer than 11 characters, use a shortened version for this exercise. If the disk already has a label, the Label text box will display it. (If you then key a new label, the new name will replace the former name.)

4. Click on the OK command button to record the label (if you do not wish to label your disk, click on the Cancel button to close the dialog box with no further action.)

5. Verify that the disk label is displayed on the Directory Tree window below the disk drive icon bar (see Figure 3.20).

6. Double-click on the File Manager Control-menu box; then click on the OK command button to close File Manager.

7. Exit Windows.

SUMMARY

This session presented you with an introduction to the File Manager, one of the most powerful and useful Windows tools. What makes the File Manager so important? The File Manager affects the basic ways in which you save and organize and view every file you create in Windows. Only by knowing and using the File Manager correctly can you get the maximum benefit from the power of Windows. In fact, the more you use Windows, the more important it is for you to understand the File Manager. For this reason, you will learn more about the File Manager in the next session.

OBJECTIVES

When you complete this session, you will be able to:

- Name, rename, copy, move, and delete directories and files.
- Create directories and subdirectories.
- Control file displays.
- Search a directory or a disk.
- Search using wildcard characters.
- Select and deselect files.

FILE MANAGER PART II

. . . .

VIEWS
Managing Directories and Files
Manipulating Directories and Files

FILE MANAGER - PART II

PREVIEW

Now that you are familiar with the File Manager window and the Directory Tree, turn your attention to the File Manager's most important tasks—manipulating directories and files.

Understanding Directory and File Names

There are rules, of course, for naming files and directories. Knowing and applying these rules will help you organize your directories and find your files. If you have some experience with computers, perhaps you are familiar with DOS (**d**isk **o**perating **s**ystem). If so, you have a head start in using the File Manager to name directories, find files, and more.

First of all, as shown in Figure 4.1, a directory name or filename consists of three parts: a *name* (from 1 to 8 characters long), a *separator*,

Figure 4.1

Directory/filename conventions

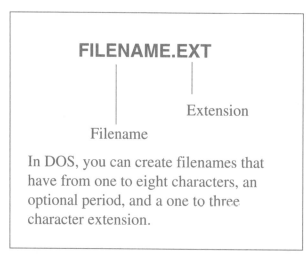

FILENAME.EXT

Extension

Filename

In DOS, you can create filenames that have from one to eight characters, an optional period, and a one to three character extension.

and an *extension* (no more than 3 characters long). For example, the filename LETTER.DOC includes the name LETTER, a separator (a period), and the extension DOC. You *must* name your files, but file extensions are optional (Windows programs add their own file extensions to filenames).

You can use any letter of the alphabet, any number, and some symbols in your names, but you cannot use a space—use a hyphen (-) or an underscore (_) instead. And remember, no more than 8 characters.

Creating Directories and Subdirectories

Directories provide a structure for organizing files into meaningful *groups* of files that you can locate and access quickly.

Think of a **directory** as a file drawer that holds a group of file folders on one subject, each folder labeled for certain kinds of files. You might have a drawer (a **directory**) labeled 1990TAX, another labeled 1991TAX, and so on for each year. In each drawer you might have different folders (**subdirectories**) labeled RETURNS, RECEIPTS, and so on. In each folder you might have dozens of papers (**files**), all related. Now, to appreciate the value of directories and subdirectories, imagine having *no* file drawers and *no* folders—just a mess of loose papers!

In File Manager, you can create directories and subdirectories when you are in the Directory Tree window or a directory window. First, what is the difference between a directory and a subdirectory? A directory comes straight from the root (that is, from A:\ or B:\ or C:\, for example), but a *sub*directory comes from a directory. In the next exercise, you will create a directory with two subdirectories beneath it. The directory comes from the root—A:\ or B:\, depending on which drive you put your *Quick Start* disk in. The two subdirectories come from the directory—that's why they are called *sub*directories.

In either case, the process of creating a directory or a subdirectory is the same. First, you must make a decision. If you are creating a directory, decide on the disk where you will place the new directory. If you are creating a subdirectory, decide under which parent directory you will place the new subdirectory. Then, whether you are creating a directory or a subdirectory, you pull down the File menu and select the Create Directory... option. The Create Directory dialog box, shown in Figure 4.2, will show you where the new directory or subdirectory will be placed. Above the Name box in Figure 4.2 you see "Current directory is A:\." If you key a name in the Name text box and click on the OK command button, you will create a directory. If, on the other hand, the line above the name box said "Current directory is C:\1991TAX," you would be creating a subdirectory beneath the 1991TAX directory, which comes from the root C:\.

Figure 4.2

Create Directory dialog box

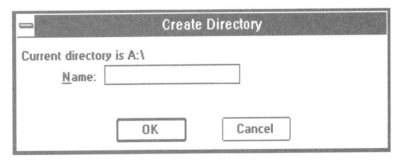

EXERCISE 4 ● 1 CREATING DIRECTORIES AND SUBDIRECTORIES

1. Launch Windows if it is not already started. Double-click on the File Manager icon.

2. Verify that your *Quick Start* disk is in one of the floppy drives. Then select that drive.

3. Select the Create Directory... option from the File menu.

4. Key the directory name *DTP* (for **d**esk**t**op **p**ublishing) in the Name text box. You can use lowercase letters; File Manager will convert them to all-capital letters.

5. Click on the OK command button. Notice that the root directory of your *Quick Start* disk now displays with a minus sign (-).

6. Select the DTP directory.

7. Select the Create Directory... option from the File menu.

8. Key the name *STORIES* in the Name text box; then click on the OK command button.

9. Click on the DTP directory icon to expand the directory. Verify that the Stories directory icon has been created.

10. Select the DTP directory icon to collapse the directory tree one level. The DTP icon should remain selected.

11. Select the Create Directory option from the File menu.

12. Key the name *GRAPHICS* in the Name text box; then click on the OK command button.

13. Click on the DTP directory to expand the directory.

Controlling File Displays

So far, we have used File Manager's defaults to display directories and files. But at times, you may want to change the display format—for example, when you are searching for a particular file or group of files. The View menu options, shown in Figure 4.3, allow you to control how files are displayed in a listing.

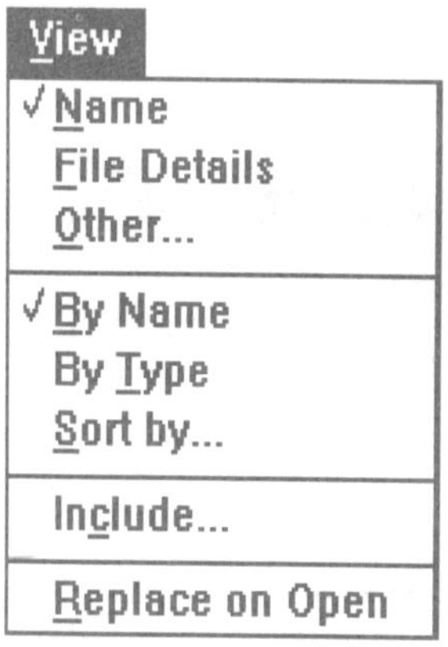

Figure 4.3

View menu

```
┌─────────────────────┐
│ View                │
├─────────────────────┤
│ √ Name              │
│   File Details      │
│   Other...          │
├─────────────────────┤
│ √ By Name           │
│   By Type           │
│   Sort by...        │
├─────────────────────┤
│   Include...        │
├─────────────────────┤
│   Replace on Open   │
└─────────────────────┘
```

The first three options control the type and the amount of information that will be displayed.

Name. This is the default option. When the Name option is selected, only directory names and filenames are listed.

File Details. When this option is selected, the display will show not only the filename but also the file size, date and time stamp, and file attributes.

Other.... This option allows you to display one or more of the file details in addition to the filename.

The next three View options determine how the file list will be sorted.

By Name. This option sorts files in normal alphabetic order by filename (with symbols first, then numbers, and finally letters). Subdirectories will be placed before files following this same sequence.

By Type. This option displays files first by alphabetic order, then by extension, and then by filename within each extension group.

Sort by. This option allows you to specify how you want the directory listing arranged. This option offers you the choice of name, type, file size, or date and time stamp.

The last two menu options permit you to control the contents and the display of directory windows.

Include.... This option allows you to select which files are to be displayed. Check boxes are displayed that allow you to display or hide directories, programs, documents, and data files.

Replace on Open. This option leaves only two windows remaining open—a Directory Tree and a directory window. When you open a new directory, the new contents replace the previous contents.

Now that you know all these options, you can control file displays in a listing—a handy tool for searching a directory or a disk.

Searching a Directory or Disk

To locate a directory or a file, you use the Search... option on the File menu. Search allows you to locate (1) one file among many within a directory, (2) one directory among many on a disk, (3) all the directories and files with similar names, or (4) all the files with a common extension.

When you select the Search... command, the Search dialog box is displayed (see Figure 4.4). If you are searching for a specific file, key the name in the

Figure 4.4

Search dialog box

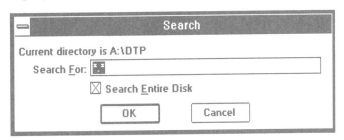

name in the Search For text box. If you do not know the exact name, or want to search for a group of files, you can use the aster-isk (*) as a wildcard character. This is explained in more detail later in this view. If you select Search Entire Disk (or simply allow the X to remain in this box) and then click on the OK button, File Manager will search the entire disk for the directory or file. If you do not select Search Entire Disk, the search will be limited to the currently selected directory.

EXERCISE 4 ● 2   SEARCHING AN ENTIRE DISK FOR A SPECIFIC FILE

Locate the PBRUSH.EXE file, which is stored in the Windows directory.

1. Select drive C (or the drive that contains the Windows directory).

2. Select the Search... option from the File menu.

3. Key the filename and extension *PBRUSH.EXE* in the Search For text box.

4. Verify that the Search Entire Disk check box is selected.

5. Click on the OK command button to start the search.

File Manager will search the entire drive C for all files that match the search specifications. When the search operation is completed, a Search Results window similar to the one illustrated in Figure 4.5 will display with an icon and the complete directory path for each file that matches your search specifications.

As Illustrated in Figure 4.5, only one match was found. The directory path C:\WINDOWS\PBRUSH.EXE indicates that the PBRUSH.EXE file is located in the WINDOWS directory on drive C.

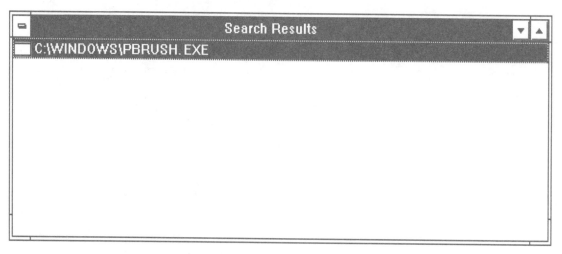

Figure 4.5 Search Results window

6. Double-click on the Control-menu box of the Search Results window to close the window.

Using Wildcards

When you do not know (or remember) the exact name or extension, you can use the wildcard character * to assist you with your search. In File Manager, an asterisk (*) means "any filename" or "any extension," depending upon where you place the asterisk. Note these four examples:

1. If you know the filename (README) but not the extension, you would enter README.* in the Search For text box.

2. If you know the extension (TXT) but not the filename, you would enter *.TXT in the Search For text box.

3. If you know a portion of the filename (READ) but not the entire name, you would enter READ*.* in the Search For text box.

4. If you know neither the filename nor the extension, enter two asterisks separated with a period (*.*) in the Search For text box. This instructs File Manager to search for all files, regardless of filename or extension.

EXERCISE 4 ● 3   SEARCHING WITH WILDCARDS

Use the wildcard character feature to locate all the files in the Windows directory that have an .EXE extension.

1. Select the Search... option from the File menu.

2. Key the filename wildcard and extension *.EXE* in the Search For text box.

3. Verify that the Search Entire Disk check box is checked.

4. Click on the OK command button to start the search.

The Search Results dialog box now lists every file that matches the search specifications. The number of files located will display at the bottom of the File Manager window.

5. Double-click on the Search Results window's control-menu box to close the window.

Selecting Directories and Files

The first step in copying, deleting, or renaming a directory or file is to *select* its icon. When you are in the Directory Tree, you can select only one directory; however, when you are in a directory window, you can select single or multiple directories and files.

A number of techniques are available that allow you to select multiple directories or files:

- To select a single directory or file, you would click on it.

- If the files are randomly scattered through the directory, you would press and *hold down* **[Ctrl]** while you click on each of the desired files. As shown in Figure 4.6, the selected files will be highlighted.

- When the files are consecutive, you would press and *hold down* **[Shift]** while you click on the first file and then click on the last file to be included. Again, the selected files will be highlighted.

- Another technique is you would use the Include... option on the View menu and the Select All option from the File menu.

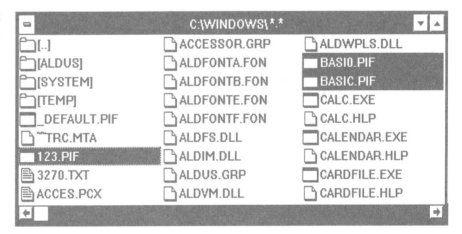

Figure 4.6

Selected multiple files with .PIF extensions

EXERCISE 4 • 4 SELECTING FILES

Selecting Individual Files

Since the techniques for manipulating both directories and files are the same, the exercises in this view use files only.

1. Scroll the Directory Tree until the Windows directory is in view.

2. Double-click on the Windows icon to display the Windows directory window.

3. Select the first file in the directory listing with a .PIF extension by clicking once on it.

4. Press and *hold down* [Ctrl]; then click on each of the remaining files in the directory listing with a .PIF extension.

5. Cancel the first file selected by pressing **[Ctrl]** and clicking on the file icon.

When you want to cancel all the selections in a directory window, use the Deselect All option from the File menu.

6. Select the Deselect All command from the File menu to deselect the selected files. One filename will remain selected.

Selecting Multiple Adjacent Files

In this part of the exercise, you will select all files with a .TXT extension. Use the View menu to make them easier to locate.

7. Select the Include... option from the View menu. Notice the directory display changes. The Include dialog box lists the file parameters you can select to include in the display.

8. Key the wildcard and extension *.TXT*; then click on the OK command button. Notice that only those files with the extension .TXT are displayed.

9. Click on the first file in the listing.

10. Press and *hold down* **[Shift]**; then click on the last file in the listing. All the intervening files will be selected, as illustrated in Figure 4.7.

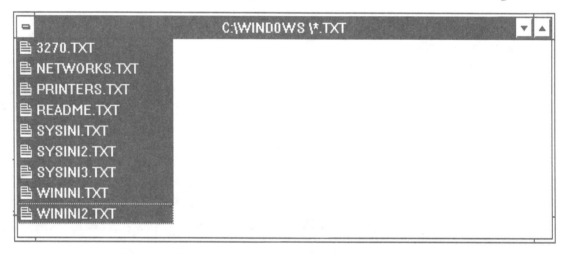

Figure 4.7 Selected multiple files with .TXT extensions

11. Select the Deselect All option from the File menu to deselect the files.

Selecting Files Using View Menu and File Menu Options

12. Select the Include... option from the View menu.

13. Key *.SYS* in the Name text box to indicate you wish to include only those files with an .SYS extension.

14. Click on the OK command button. Only those files with the desired extension will be displayed.

15. Select the Select All option from the File menu. All the files in the directory window should be selected, as illustrated in Figure 4.8.

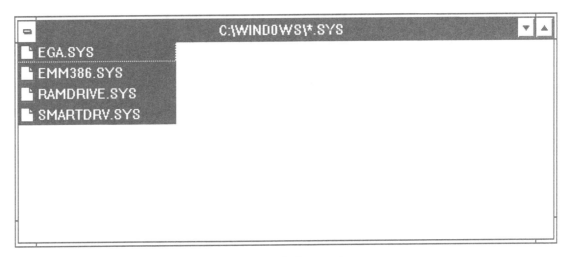

Figure 4.8 Selected files with .SYS extension

Deselecting Files and Closing Directories

Once you have selected the desired files, you can manipulate them by issuing various commands. Manipulating techniques will be presented in the next view. For now, deselect the files and close all open directories.

16. Select the Deselect All option from the File menu. All files are deselected.

17. Select the Close All Directories option from the Window menu to return to the Directory Tree.

VIEW 2

MANIPULATING DIRECTORIES AND FILES

PREVIEW

You have seen how File Manager permits you to organize and manage files, directories, and disks, but the real power of File Manager lies in its ability to *manipulate* directories and files. Unless you never make a mistake or never change your mind, at times you will need to erase unwanted directories and files, copy files to other disks, or move files between directories and disks. File Manager is an excellent tool for performing these operations.

Displaying Warning Messages

During some File Manager operations, you are given the option of displaying a warning message that asks if, for example, you really want to delete a file. Because they give you an opportunity to change your mind before executing certain commands, warning messages are obviously important; once deleted, a directory or file may be lost forever. On the other hand, too many confirmation messages are annoying. In File Manager, the choice is yours. To turn off selected warning messages, check the appropriate boxes in the Confirmation dialog box (see Figure 4.9).

Figure 4.9

Confirmation dialog box

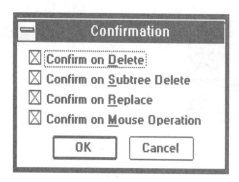

To access the Confirmation dialog box, pull down the Options menu and select Confirmation. You will see the following options:

Check this . . .	To get confirmation of . . .
Confirm on Delete	Each file being erased
Confirm on Subtree Delete	Each directory being erased
Confirm on Replace	One file being placed over another with the same name
Confirm on Mouse Operation	Moving or copying any directory or file using the mouse

Copying Directories and Files

Files are copied *from* a "source" *to* a "destination." Whenever you need to copy directories or files, make both the source and the destination directory window visible. In this way, you can see what you are copying and where it is going. If the source and the destination are on different disks, tile the directory windows, as illustrated in Figure 4.10.

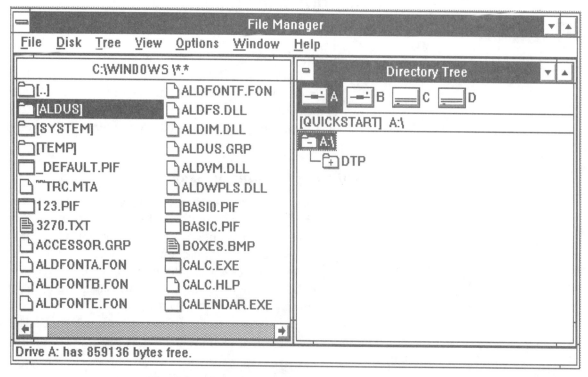

Figure 4.10 Source and destination directory windows displayed in the tile format

When both source and destination are in view, select the file or directory to be copied (the source). You can select more than one, as described earlier in this session. Then use the mouse to drag the selected file or directory to its destination, the directory window where you want the copy to be placed. If the destination is on the same disk, press and hold down **[Ctrl]** as you drag the file.

When using a mouse, you can release the icon of the copied directory or file on top of another directory window, on top of a directory icon in the Directory Tree, on top of a directory icon at the bottom of the File Manager window, or on top of a disk drive icon at the top of the File Manager.

Now, copy all the graphic files in the Windows directory with the extension .BMP to the GRAPHICS directory on your *Quick Start* disk.

EXERCISE 4 ● 5 COPYING FILES

1. Place your *Quick Start* disk in one of the floppy drives.

2. Open the Windows directory window (the source).

3. Select the Tile option from the Window menu.

4. Select the drive (from the Directory Tree window) in which you have placed your *Quick Start* disk.

5. Select the Expand All option from the Tree Menu to display the Graphics subdirectory (destination).

6. Select the Windows directory window.

7. Select the Include... option on the View menu.

8. Key the wildcard and extension *.*BMP* in the text box, and click on the OK command button.

Only those files with a .BMP extension will be displayed in the Windows directory window.

9. Select the Select All option from the File menu.

10. Point anywhere in the highlighted area, press the mouse button, and then move the mouse slightly. The cursor will change into a graphic that looks like a stack of cards.

11. Continue to hold down the mouse button and drag the graphic across the screen until it sits on top of the Graphics directory icon. Release the mouse button. A dialog box asks you to confirm that you want to copy the files into the directory (Figure 4.11).

Figure 4.11

Confirm Mouse Operation message box

12. Click on the Yes button to copy the files.

Moving Directories and Files

Moving a directory or file is similar to copying—the difference is that the Move command removes the directory or file from its original location.

EXERCISE 4 • 6   MOVING FILES

1. Open the Graphics subdirectory window on your *Quick Start* disk.

2. Select the WEAVE.BMP file (the source). Be sure you select *only* this file.

3. Select the Tile option on the Window menu.

4. Press and hold down **[Alt]**; then drag the WEAVE.BMP file icon from the GRAPHICS subdirectory window and place it on top of the Stories subdirectory. The thin rule will surround the directory icon when you are at the correct position.

5. Release the mouse button and **[Alt]** when the icon is over the directory.

6. Click on the Yes button to move the file.

7. Select the Close All Directories option on the Window menu. The Directory Tree window will remain open.

Renaming Directories and Files

File Manager has a simple process for renaming directories and files: Select the source, issue the Rename... command, key the new name in the Rename dialog box, and then click on the Rename command button.

EXERCISE 4 • 7   RENAMING FILES

Renaming a Single File

1. Select the drive containing the *Quick Start* disk. Then click on the DTP directory icon.

2. Select the Rename... option from the File menu.

3. Key the new name *DESKTOP* in the text box; then click on the Rename command button.

4. Expand the Directory Tree to verify the name change.

Renaming Multiple Files

5. Double-click on the Graphics subdirectory icon to open the directory window.

6. Select the Select All option from the File menu.

7. Select the Rename... option from the File menu.

8. Key the new name *.GRA* in the text box, and click on the Rename command button.

9. Verify that the files have been renamed.

Deleting Directories and Files

With File Manager, you can delete one file or a large group of files in a single action. But note that when you delete a directory or a subdirectory name, you also delete *all* the files in it! For this reason, you should select the Confirm on Delete box *and* the Confirm on Subtree Delete box (see Confirmation... on the Options menu).

EXERCISE 4 • 8   DELETING FILES

Delete all the files in the Graphics directory. Although you usually want to select the Confirm on Delete box, to speed up this activity, you will deselect this warning message in this exercise only.

1. Select the Confirmation... option from the Options menu to bring up the Confirmation dialog box.

2. Deselect (uncheck) the Confirm on Delete option by clicking on the check box. Leave the other check boxes selected (checked).

3. Click on the OK command button.

4. Select the first filename in this window; then press **[Shift]** and click on the last filename.

5. Select the Delete... option from the File menu to erase the selected files; then click on the Delete command button. The files will be deleted.

6. Double-click on the Control-menu box of the Graphics directory window to close the directory window.

7. Double-click File Manager's Control-menu box to close File Manager. Verify that the Save Settings check box is *un*checked before you click on the OK command button.

SUMMARY

In this session you witnessed the power of the File Manager to organize, display, control, and manipulate files and directories. In the exercises in this session you gained experience in creating, naming, renaming, copying, moving, and deleting directories and subdirectories, as well as in controlling file displays and searching a directory or a disk. This experience will prove very valuable and will enable you to use Windows productively and efficiently!

• • • • • • • • • • • • •

OBJECTIVES

When you complete this session, you will be able to:

- Explain the purpose and value of using the Windows desktop accessories.

- Create, edit, save, and print a Notepad document.

- Copy and move text using the Clipboard.

- Insert, delete, replace, copy, and move text in a Notepad document.

- Use the Calculator to perform basic arithmetic computations.

- Maintain an appointment calendar, set message reminders, and print daily appointment pages in the Windows Calendar.

- Create, maintain, and utilize a Cardfile to retrieve stored information.

SESSION 5

· · · · · · · · · · · · · · · ·

DESKTOP ACCESSORIES

DESKTOP ACCESSORIES

A major feature of Windows is that it can run several programs simultaneously. For example, Windows comes with a number of helpful desktop accessory applications that are designed to be used *while* you are working in a program application—that's why they are called **accessory applications**. Thus, while working in *Word for Windows*, you could use the Calculator accessory to add a column of numbers; while in *Excel* for Windows, you could use the Notepad accessory to jot down a short note or reminder. Equally important, desktop accessories do not use much computer memory.

In this session, you will learn to use the Notepad, the Calculator, the Calendar, and the Cardfile. In later sessions, you will learn to use Write (a word processing program) and Paintbrush (a graphic illustration program). All of the accessories are located in the Accessories group window.

VIEW 1

THE NOTEPAD

PREVIEW

Notepad lets you create simple notes, quick reminders, records of phone calls, and daily "to do" lists. Notepad is *not* used to create long, complex documents. Notepad saves files as ASCII (**A**merican **S**tandard **C**ode for **I**nformation **I**nterchange) that most word processing software "understands." Therefore, almost all word processing software can accept Notepad files. Also, Notepad can be used to create and edit the ASCII files used by your computer's operating system.

Starting Notepad and Keying Text

To start Notepad, you will double-click on the Notepad icon in the Accessories group window. You are able to begin keying your exercise immediately, but before you do, look at the Notepad window in Figure 5.1. The window shows the Notepad menu bar, with its four options: File, Edit, Search, and Help. Just below the word *File*, note the cursor, a thin vertical line that indicates the **insertion point**, the place where text will be entered when keyed. On screen, the cursor appears as a blinking line. When you enter text, each character you key will appear to the left of the cursor.

You can move around the Notepad window in several ways using the mouse or the keyboard. Let's review the use of these two devices.

Moving around Notepad with the mouse:

1. To move up or down the page, click on the arrows at either end of the *vertical* scroll bar.

2. To move the page to the left or right, click on either end of the *horizontal* scroll bar.

3. To move the cursor anywhere on the screen, position the mouse arrow and then click.

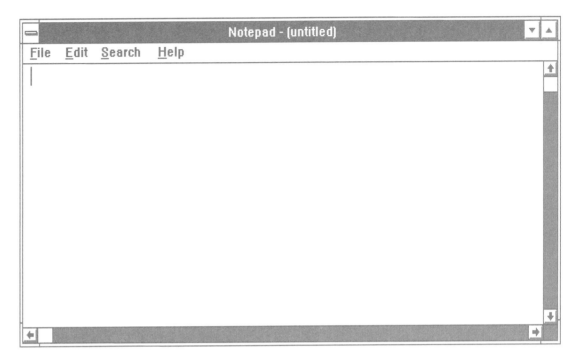

Figure 5.1 Notepad window

Moving around Notepad with the keyboard:

1. Scroll a page by pressing **[Pg Up]** or **[Pg Dn]**.

2. Scroll one line at a time by pressing the up arrow or down arrow.

You cannot move beyond the end of the document. Before you continue, look at Figure 5.2, which shows all the options on the File, Edit, and Search menus. Note especially the Word Wrap option in the Edit menu (other options will be discussed later). Notepad does not automatically word wrap. (**Word wrap** means that the computer makes end-of-line breaks for you). With Notepad, you must select the Word Wrap option; then the text will fit the width of the Notepad window. In Figure 5.3, the smaller window shows the results of selecting the Word Wrap option. Or if you prefer, you can indicate your own line breaks by pressing **[Enter]**. Otherwise, Notepad continues text across the screen.

Figure 5.2

File, Edit, and Search menus expanded

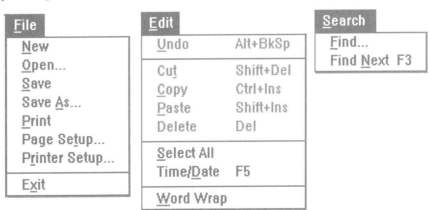

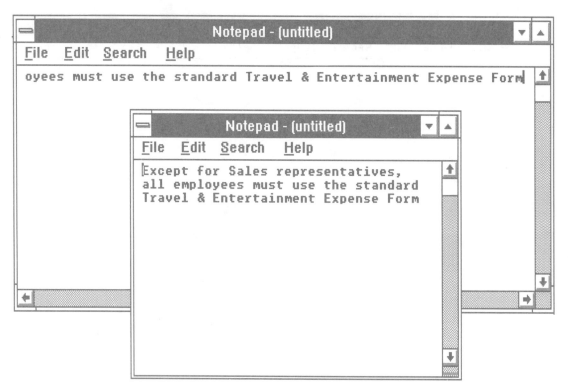

Figure 5.3 Wide window with text and smaller window with same text wrapped

EXERCISE 5 ● 1   STARTING NOTEPAD AND KEYING TEXT

1. Start Windows, if it is not currently running.

2. Click on the Accessories window to activate it.

3. Double-click on the Notepad icon to open a Notepad window.

4. Select the Word Wrap option from the Edit menu.

5. Key text:

　　a. Use the **[Backspace]** or the **[Delete]** key to correct keying errors as necessary.

　　b. Press **[Enter]** only at the end of a paragraph, not at the end of each line. Let Notepad word wrap the text for you.

　　c. Now key the following text:

　　　Because Notepad creates files, you can open and edit Windows system files and other text files. Text files generally have a BAT, INI, or TXT file extension.

　　　A Notepad document can hold nearly 50,000 characters, about eight to ten pages. The About Notepad option on the Help menu will tell you how many characters are in a file.

Saving and Printing a Notepad Document

You can save Notepad documents on disk and print the files on paper (called a **hard copy**). To save documents, use the Save and Save As...

options on the File menu (both are discussed in greater detail in Session 6, in the discussion on Windows Write). Then use the Print option on the File menu to print a document.

EXERCISE 5 • 2 SAVING AND PRINTING A NOTEPAD DOCUMENT

1. Insert your *Quick Start* data disk in one of the floppy disk drives.

2. Select the Save As... command from the File Menu.

3. Select the drive that contains your *Quick Start* disk.

4. Select the DESKTOP subdirectory.

5. Select the STORIES subdirectory in the DESKTOP directory.

6. Key the filename *NOTEPAD* in the Filename text box; then click on the OK command button. Notepad will automatically assign your file a .TXT extension. If you want a different extension, key it along with the filename.

If you have a printer attached to your computer system, you can print a copy of your document. If you do not have a printer, you will not be able to complete steps 7 and 8 in this exercise.

7. Select the Print option from the File menu.

8. Click on the OK command button to print the document. Inspect the printed document.

Inserting, Deleting, and Replacing Text

Notepad offers a number of features to help you edit your documents. For example, with Notepad you can:

• *Add* characters by moving the cursor to the desired location, clicking the mouse button, and then keying the text.

• *Delete* characters by pressing the **[Del]** or the **[Backspace]** key, depending on the position of the cursor.

• *Replace* characters by keying new text over old text. First, select or highlight the undesired text by clicking an insertion point to left of the location where the replacement is to go; then click the mouse button and drag the mouse across the undesired text. The next character keyed will delete the highlighted text.

EXERCISE 5 • 3 INSERTING, DELETING, AND REPLACING TEXT

1. Click an insertion point immediately after the letter "s" in the word "creates" in the first line of text.

2. Press **[Spacebar]** once; then key the word *text.*

3. Click an insertion point immediately following the letter "d" in the word "and" near the end of the first line of text.

4. Press **[Backspace]** nine times to remove the letters, "d," "n," "a," and "space"; then remove the letters "n," "e," "p," and "o" and the space following the letter "o."

5. Click an insertion point immediately before the letter "n" in the word "nearly" in the first sentence of the second paragraph.

6. Press and hold down the mouse button; then drag across the text "nearly" to select it.

7. Key the text *almost.* Notice that the keyed text replaced the original text.

8. Select the Print option from the File menu.

9. Click on the OK command button. Inspect your document when it comes out of the printer.

Copying and Moving Text Using the Clipboard

Notepad's Edit menu, shown in Figure 5.4, offers a number of additional options for editing text. For example, to copy text, highlight the text, select Copy from the Edit menu, position the cursor where you want the copy to go, and then select Paste from the Edit menu. It's that simple. And to move text, use Cut and Paste (instead of Copy and Paste). (Edit options are discussed in greater detail in Session 6, Windows Write).

Figure 5.4

Notepad's Edit menu

Edit	
Undo	Alt+BkSp
Cut	Shift+Del
Copy	Ctrl+Ins
Paste	Shift+Ins
Delete	Del
Select All	
Time/Date	F5
Word Wrap	

EXERCISE 5 • 4   COPYING AND MOVING TEXT USING THE CLIPBOARD

Copying Text

1. Click an insertion point immediately before the letter "A," the first word in the first line of the second paragraph.

2. Press the mouse button and drag across the sentence up to and including the two spaces following the period to select the sentence.

3. Select the Copy option from the Edit menu. The text is copied to the Clipboard (a storage area in the computer's memory).

4. Click an insertion point immediately following the period at the end of the second paragraph.

5. Press **[Spacebar]** twice.

6. Select the Paste option from the Edit menu. The text is copied from the Clipboard and pasted to your document.

Moving Text

7. Click an insertion point immediately before the first word in the first paragraph ("Because").

8. Drag to select the entire paragraph (up to and including the word "extension").

9. Select the Cut option from the Edit menu. The selected text is cut from the document and placed on the Clipboard.

10. Click an insertion point immediately following the last word in the last paragraph.

11. Press **[Enter]** twice to create a blank line after the last word.

12. Select the Paste option from the Edit menu.

13. Select the Print option from the File menu.

14. Click on the OK command button. Inspect your document when it comes out of the printer.

Searching a Notepad Document

Using the Search menu, you can quickly locate words and phrases in a Notepad document. Click an insertion point, then search the document in either a forward or a backward direction.

EXERCISE 5 ● 5   SEARCHING A NOTEPAD DOCUMENT

1. Click an insertion point immediately before the first word in the document.

2. Select the Find... option from the Search menu.

3. Key the text to be located, *files*, in the Find What text box.

4. Verify that the Forward button is selected; then click on the OK command button.

   When Notepad finds the first occurrence of the word *files*, it stops the search and highlights the word.

5. Select the Find... option from the Search menu.

6. Verify that the search word *files* is shown in the Find What text box; then click on the OK command button. The search will begin again, this time starting at the last occurrence of the word.

7. Select the Find Next option from the Search menu to search the remaining text. Select the Find Next option again. When Notepad finds no more occurrences of the search word, it shows a message box indicating that no match was found (Figure 5.5).

Figure 5.5

Search message box

Closing Notepad

Notepad can be closed in either of two ways:

- By opening a new file
- By closing the Notepad program.

To open a file, select the Open... option from the File menu. To close or quit Notepad, select the Exit option from the File menu. Remember to save your file first.

EXERCISE 5 • 6   CLOSING NOTEPAD

1. Select the Save option from the File menu.

2. Select the Exit option from the File menu.

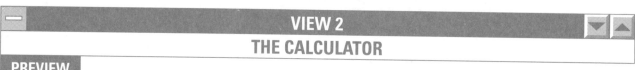

VIEW 2

THE CALCULATOR

PREVIEW

On screen, the Windows Calculator appears in its own window, its title bar labeled Calculator, of course. As shown in Figure 5.6, the Calculator menu bar has Edit, View, and Help options. You can minimize the calculator to an icon, but there is no maximize button; the Calculator window cannot be resized.

You can use either the mouse or the keyboard to operate the Calculator. The numeric keypad (to the right of your alphabetic keyboard) functions like a standard ten-key calculator. Just turn on **[Num Lock]**; the numeric keypad will then be active.

Figure 5.6

The Calculator window

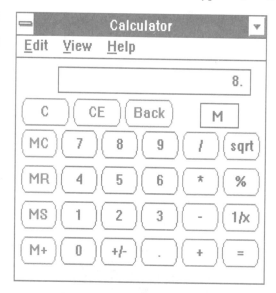

In addition to standard calculations (addition, subtraction, multiplication, and division), the Calculator can compute square roots, percentages, reciprocals, and more. The Calculator has a memory for storing data, and it can be configured as a scientific calculator capable of very complex operations. The scientific calculator works the same as the standard calculator but contains many advanced features. (Since these features are beyond the scope of *Quick Start*, only the standard calculator will be discussed.)

Opening and Closing the Calculator

Open the Calculator by double-clicking on its icon in the Accessories group window. Whether the Calculator opens in the standard or the scientific mode depends on its last setting. To change the mode, select the standard or scientific option from the View menu. Close the Calculator by clicking on the Control-menu box and selecting the Close option.

EXERCISE 5 • 7   OPENING THE CALCULATOR AND SELECTING A VIEW

1. Double-click on the Calculator icon to open the Calculator window.

2. Select the Scientific option from the View menu. Notice that the scientific calculator has more buttons than a standard handheld calculator.

3. Select the Standard option from the View menu.

Using the Standard Calculator

To operate the Calculator, press the appropriate buttons, using either the mouse or the numeric keypad and keyboard. This is one Windows application when the mouse is *not* easier than the keyboard! When using a mouse, select number and function keys on the Calculator by clicking on the appropriate keys. Numbers appear in the display window as you select them or as the Calculator computes them.

When using the numeric keypad, just press the appropriate numbers. To edit the display or perform calculations using the keyboard or a mouse, note these instructions:

To. . .	**Using the Keyboard** *Press. . .*	**Using the Mouse** *Click On. . .*
Add	[+]	+
Subtract	[-]	-
Multiply	[*]	*
Divide	[/]	/
Clear (erase) the memory	[Esc]	C
Clear last function or displayed number	[Delete]	CE
Delete the last number in the displayed value	[Backspace]	Back
Clear the Calculation	[Esc]	C
Add displayed number to memory	[Ctrl] + [P]	M+
Clear memory	[Ctrl] + [C]	MC
Recall value from memory	[Ctrl] + [R]	MR
Store value in memory	[Ctrl] + [M]	MS
Take square root of displayed number		

The simplest way to learn to use the Calculator is to do a few exercises using the keypad and the keyboard.

EXERCISE 5 . 8   MAKING SIMPLE CALCULATIONS

Addition

1. Compute the sum of 4 + 2.

    a. Key **[4]** then **[+]**. The number "4" should appear in the display.

    b. Key **[2]** then **[=]**. The answer "6" should appear in the display.

Subtraction

2. Compute the remainder 100 - 60.

    a. Key **[1] [0] [0]** then **[-]**. The number "100" will appear in the display.

    b. Key **[6] [0]** then **[=]**. The answer "40" will appear in the display.

Multiplication

3. Compute the product of 50 x 3.

    a. Key **[5] [0]** then **[*]**. The number "50" will appear in the display.

    b. Key **[3]** then **[=]**. The answer "150" will appear in the display.

Division

4. Compute the quotient of 100 / 25 (100 divided by 25).

    a. Key **[1] [0] [0]** then **[/]**. The number "100" will appear in the display.

    b. Key **[2] [5]** then **[=]**. The answer "4" will appear in the display.

EXERCISE 5 . 9   MAKING MORE COMPLEX CALCULATIONS

Calculating Percents

1. Find 28% of 75.

    a. Key **[7] [5]** then **[*]**. The number "75" will appear in the display.

    b. Key **[2] [8]** then **[%]**. The answer "21" will appear in the display.

    c. Press **[ESC]** to clear all numbers and functions. You must always clear the calculator display after computing a percentage.

Computing Square Roots

2. Find the square root of 144.

    a. Key **[1] [4] [4]**.

    b. Press **[@]**. The answer "12" will appear in the display.

    c. Press **[ESC]** to clear all numbers and functions.

Using Memory Functions

The memory buttons permit you to save a number in the calculator's memory. When you put a number in memory, an M will appear in the display box just under and to the right of the number display, as shown in Figure 5.7.

Figure 5.7

The Calculator with M in display

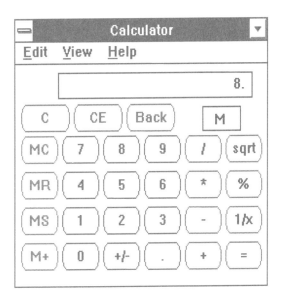

To put a number in memory, select the number in the display, and then click on the M+ button. If you want to save the result of a calculated number, click on the MS (memory store) button once the result is calculated. The stored number can be recalled from memory by clicking on the MR (memory recall) button.

EXERCISE 5 • 10   USING MEMORY FUNCTIONS

1. Compute the sum of (15 x 23) + (224 / 16).

    a. Key **[1] [5]** then **[*]**; key **[2] [3]** then **[=]**. The answer "345" will appear in the display.

    b. Key **[CTRL] + [P]**. The letter "M" appears in the display window along with the number "345."

    c. Key **[2] [2] [4]** then **[/]**; key **[1] [6]** then **[=]**. The answer "14" appears in the display.

    d. Key **[CTRL] + [P]**. The "14" remains in the display.

    e. Key **[CTRL] + [R]**. The number "359" is shown in the display.

    f. Key **[CTRL] + [C]** to clear the memory and display.

2. Double-click on the Control-menu box to close the calculator.

VIEW 3
THE CALENDAR

PREVIEW

The Windows Calendar is designed to support your appointment book or diary. You can set an almost indefinite number of alarms (audible or visual) minutes, hours, days, even years in advance. When Calendar is opened, an untitled calendar book (Figure 5.8) appears.

The Calendar window has all the standard window elements. The Calendar menu bar shows seven menus: File, Edit, View, Show, Alarm, Options, and Help. The status line below the Menu bar displays the current time (according to your computer's internal clock) and the calendar date.

Beneath the status line an appointment page is displayed in either Day view or Month view. The appointment page is designed for recording events by time, day, and date. The scroll arrows on the status bar let you

Figure 5.8

The Calendar window

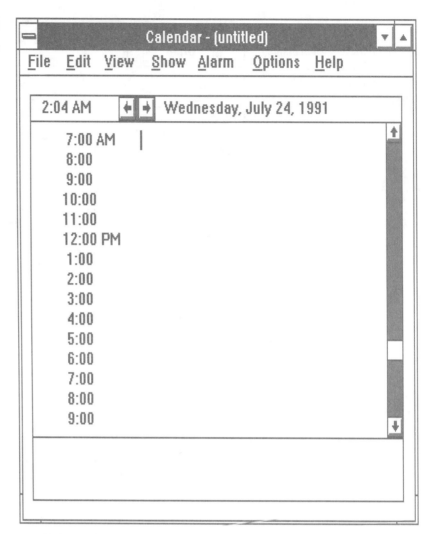

scroll through the pages by date.   Finally, at the bottom of the Calendar below the appointment area is a box called the **scratch pad**.

EXERCISE 5 ● 11   OPENING THE CALENDAR AND CHANGING ITS VIEW

1. Start Windows if it is not currently running.

2. Click on the Accessories window to activate it.

3. Double-click on the Calendar icon to open a Calendar window.

4. Select the Month view option from the View menu.

5. Select the Day view option from the View menu.

Making and Tracking Appointments

To record appointments in the time slots on the calendar page, click an insertion point at the correct time and then key the entry. Each line will hold about 80 characters. If you wish to make an appointment at a time other than one listed on the page, add a new time slot or change the time increments on the entire page to add more time slots.

To add a new time slot, select the Special Time... option from the Options menu. When the Special Time dialog box displays, key the special time in the text box as shown in Figure 5.9; then click on the Insert

Figure 5.9

Special Time dialog box

command button. A special time can be deleted by clicking on the Delete command button after recording the time in the text box.

EXERCISE 5 ● 12   MAKING AND TRACKING APPOINTMENTS

Entering Appointments

1. Enter an 8 a.m. appointment with Sandra Collins regarding payroll records:

  a. Click an insertion point to the right of the 8:00 a.m. time slot.

  b. Key the appointment text as shown here:.

    Meeting with Sandra Collins - Payroll Records

  c. Press **[Enter]**.

2. Enter a 12 noon luncheon meeting with the Budget Committee:

  a. Click an insertion point to the right of the 12:00 p.m. time slot.

  b. Key the appointment text as shown here:

    Lunch with Budget Committee

  c. Press **[Enter]**.

Display a Different Date

3. Enter an appointment for an applicant interview at 2 p.m. one week from today.

  a. Click on the right scroll arrow on the status bar until the same day of the week, one week from today, appears displayed on the status line.

  b. Click an insertion point to the right of the 2:00 p.m. time slot.

  c. Key the appointment text as shown here:

    Joyce Findley - Applicant Interview

  d. Press **[Enter]**.

  e. Select the Date option from the Show menu; then key the current date in the text box. Use the format mm/dd/yy.

  f. Click on the OK command button.

Set an Alarm

4. Enter an appointment for 9:55 a.m. and set an alarm.

a. Select the Special Time... option from the Options menu. A Special Time dialog will display.

b. Key the time 9:55 in the text box, click on the AM button, and click on the Insert button.

c. Select the Controls... option from the Alarm menu, and verify that the Sound check box is selected; then click on the OK command button.

d. Key the appointment text as shown here:

    Call New York office

e. Select the Set option from the Alarm menu.

f. Press **[Enter]**.

5. Enter an appointment exactly five minutes from the current time.

a. Select the Special Time... option from the Options menu. A Special Time dialog will display.

b. Key the time five minutes from now in the text box, click on the appropriate time button; then click on the Insert button.

c. Key the appointment text as shown below.

    Remember to print this page.

d. Select the Set option from the Alarm menu.

e. Press **[Enter]**.

6. Record a message in the scratch pad at the bottom of the page.

a. Click an insertion point on the scratch pad and key the following note:

    (Your Name) created this calendar page.

b. Press **[Enter]**.

Saving an Appointment Book

You can create and save as many Calendar files as you need. For example, you may make a different calendar file for each person using the computer or for each project you have been assigned. Save a Calendar file as you would any other document file. You will save your appointment book on your *Quick Start* disk; so place that disk in the appropriate drive before continuing.

EXERCISE 5 • 13   SAVING AN APPOINTMENT BOOK

1. Select the Save as... option from the File menu.

2. Select the appropriate drive.

3. Click an insertion point in the Filename text box.

4. Key the name *MY_CAL* (use an underscore between the words) in the Filename text box.

5. Click on the OK command button.

Printing from an Appointment Book

You can print the appointments in your calendar book, but only from the Day view. You can print one page or a range or pages.

EXERCISE 5 • 14   PRINTING FROM AN APPOINTMENT BOOK

1. Select the Print... option from the File menu.

2. Key the appointment day for which you have been recording appointments in the From text box, if it is not already displayed in the box. (Use the format "mm/dd/yy.") Leave the To text box blank. If you want only one date, you do not need to key a date in the To text box.

3. Click on the OK command button.

EXERCISE 5 • 15   CLOSING CALENDAR AND THE CALENDAR FILE PROGRAM

1. Select the Save option from the File menu.

2. Double-click on the Control-menu of the Calendar window to close the Calendar program.

VIEW 4
THE CARDFILE

PREVIEW

The Windows Cardfile is like an electronic stack of 3-by-5 index cards. It was designed to replace the rotary-type file many individuals keep on their real desktop. Cardfile allows you to create index cards on screen, file them, sort them, review their contents, and use the information on the cards in other applications. For example, you might maintain a cardfile of names and addresses to use when creating form letters in the Write program. You can even use Cardfile to dial a telephone number you have saved in a cardfile if you have the proper equipment.

Starting Cardfile and Creating a Cardfile

To open Cardfile, double-click on its program icon—a stack of cards. You will see the familiar window elements, shown in Figure 5.10. Beneath the menu bar is a status bar, much like the one found on the Calendar. Cardfile's workspace displays an empty card with two places to enter information:

• The index line records the word or phrase that Cardfile uses when it sorts the cards.

• The information area stores the information that you key or paste in the form of text or graphics.

Figure 5.10

Cardfile window

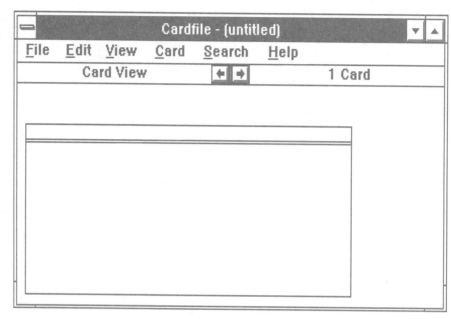

Cardfile allows you to create your file of index cards on screen and then sort, review, edit, and print cards.

EXERCISE 5 • 16   STARTING CARDFILE AND CREATING A CARDFILE

1. Double-click on the Cardfile icon to open the Cardfile accessory.

2. Create a card for James Allison of Acme Printers:

a. Key the following text at the insertion point. Press **[Enter]** after each line as shown.

Mr. James Allison
Acme Printers

(213) 555-1246
146 So. Main
Los Angeles, CA 90001

You must select the Index option before you can enter any data in this space (the blank line at the top of the index card). If you are using a mouse, you can double-click on the index line to select it.

b. Double-click on the Index line to display the Index dialog box (Figure 5.11).

Figure 5.11

Index dialog box

Index
Index Line: [   ]
OK   Cancel

c. Key the Index line text *Acme Printers* in the text box and click on the OK command button. The index line text is recorded on the index line of the card.

Adding Cards

You can add an almost limitless number of cards to an existing file by selecting the Add... option on the Card menu. When adding cards, you must key the index line before you can input any information on the body of the card. The added card will always appear in the front of the stack.

EXERCISE 5 • 17   ADDING CARDS

1. Add a card for Dorothy McMillan to the existing cardfile.

a. Select the Add... option from the Card menu. An Add dialog box is displayed.

b. Key the index line *Baker Paper Co.* and click on the OK command button. A new card with the index line you have just entered is displayed at front of the stack.

c. Key the following information in the body of the card; then click on the OK command button.

Ms. Dorothy McMillan
Baker Paper Co.

(714) 555-2364
1650 So. Broadway
Santa Ana, CA 92674

2. Add a card for Louis Chang to the existing cardfile.

a. Select the Add... option from the Card menu. An Add dialog box is displayed.

b. Key the index line, *Chang Graphics*, and click on the OK command button. The new card is displayed at front of the stack.

c. Key the following information in the body of the card; then click on the OK command button.

Mr. Louis Chang
President
Chang Graphics

(213) 555-6533
123 Los Angeles St.
Los Angeles, CA 90023

3. Add a card with your name and your school or work address. Include the text *Session 5 Exercise* on the index line.

Scrolling and Searching a Cardfile

The real value in Cardfile is the speed and the ease with which you can search for and retrieve information. There are several ways to search through a stack of cards to locate information. Three of the most commonly used methods are to:

- Scroll through the cards one by one.
- Search the cards to locate a specific card.
- Search the cards to locate a specific word or phrase.

You can scroll (look at each card one by one) the Cardfile with the scroll bar arrows. Use the left arrow to scroll backward one card at a time, and the right arrow to scroll forward one card at a time.

Use the Search menu to locate a card with specific information in the index line or body. If you want to search on the index line, use the Go To... option on the Search menu. If you want to search through the information in the body of the card, use the Find... option on the Search menu.

EXERCISE 5 • 18   SCROLLING AND SEARCHING A CARDFILE

Scrolling

1. Click on the right scroll arrow to scroll forward through the cards until the first card you entered (James Allison) is displayed at the front of the stack.

2. Click on the left scroll arrow to scroll backward one card.

Searching by Index Line

3. Select the Go To... option on the Search menu. The Search dialog box will be displayed.

4. Key the search word *Printers* in the text box and click on the OK command button. The first card found with the search word on the text line will come to the front of the stack.

Searching the Body

5. Select the Find... option on the Search menu.

6. Key the search word *Los* in the text box, and click on the OK command button. You can specify any portion of text. Here we have used just the word "Los," rather than the entire word Los Angeles.

When you know there are more cards with the search word, you can issue the Find... command again to locate the next card that contains the search word.

7. Select the Find... option on the Search menu; then click on the OK command button. You do not have to reenter the search word—it remains in the text box until changed. Also, if the search word is the same, you can also use the Find Next option form the Search menu.

Saving, Closing, and Opening a Cardfile

Save cardfiles as you would all other files—with the Save or Save As... option on the File menu. When you save a cardfile, it is automatically given the extension .CRD. You can create and save as many cardfiles as you wish, but be sure to give each one a unique name (or save files with the same names on different disks).

Close a cardfile by opening a new file or by selecting the Exit option from the File menu. You can open any existing cardfile using the Open... option on the File menu.

EXERCISE 5 ● 19 SAVING, CLOSING, AND OPENING A CARDFILE

Saving

You will need your *Quick Start* disk in order to complete the remaining exercises in this view. Before proceeding, insert your *Quick Start* disk in the appropriate disk drive.

1. Select the Save As... option from the File menu.

2. Select the appropriate drive.

3. Click an insertion point in the Filename text box.

4. Key the filename *MY_FILE* in the text box.

5. Click on the OK command button.

Opening an Existing Cardfile

6. Select the Open... option from the File menu.

7. Select the drive containing your *Quick Start* disk from the directory list on the File Open dialog box.

8. Select the file called *MY_FILE*; then click on the OK command button.

Duplicating, Editing, and Deleting Cards

You can perform all the same editing functions in the Cardfile that you can in the Notepad.

EXERCISE 5 ● 20 DUPLICATING, EDITING, AND DELETING CARDS

Duplicating and Editing

1. Add a card for Michael Jones, who works at Chang Graphics. He and Louis Chang have the same address and phone number.

   a. Select the Go to... option on the Search menu.

   b. Key the search words *Chang Graphics* in the text box and click on the OK command button. Louis Chang's card displays at the front of the stack.

c. Select the Duplicate option from the Card menu.

d. Click an insertion point in front of the name "Mr. Louis Chang" and drag to the end of the word "President." Key the name *Michael Jones.* The new name should replace the old name and title.

As shown above, body text on any card can be edited with the usual Windows text-editing procedures. If you want to edit the index line, you must select the Index... option from the Edit menu.

Deleting

2. Delete the card for James Allison at Acme Printers:

a. Select the Go To... option on the Search menu.

b. Key the search words *Acme Printers* in the text box and click on the OK command button. James Allison's card displays at the front of the stack.

c. Select the Delete option from the Card menu. A confirmation box will appear before the card is deleted.

d. Click on the OK command button to delete the card.

Printing a Cardfile

When printing cardfiles, you have the option of printing the top card only (Print option) or all the cards (Print All option). The printed cards will be the same size as standard rotary file cards.

EXERCISE 5 • 21   PRINTING A CARDFILE

1. Arrange the cards so the card with your name on it is on the top.

2. Select the Print All option from the File menu.

EXERCISE 5 • 22   CLOSING CARDFILE

1. Select the Exit option from the File menu. Respond to the confirmation message, if prompted.

Since you made a change to the cardfile (you deleted a card and moved your card to display first), a message box will display asking if you want to save changes before closing.

2. Click on the Save button to save the changes and close the file.

3. Select the Exit Windows option from the Program Manager Control-menu box.

4. Click on the OK command button to exit Windows.

SUMMARY

Windows provides a number of Desktop Accessories designed for you to use while you are working in a program application. In this session, you learned to use Notepad, Calculator, Calendar, and Cardfile.

Notepad lets you create simple notes, quick reminders, records of phone calls, and daily "to do" lists. Notepad's Edit menu allows you several options for editing text, including copying and moving text using the Clipboard.

The Windows Calculator provides standard calculations, plus the ability to compute square roots, percentages, reciprocals, and more.

The Calendar is designed to support your appointment book or diary. It can even set an indefinite number of alarms (audible or visual) minutes, hours, days, years in advance.

Finally, Cardfile is like an electronic stack of 3-by-5 index cards. It is designed to replace the rotary-type file many individuals keep on their real desktop. This accessory allows you to create index cards on screen, file them, sort them, review their contents, and use the information on the cards in other applications.

The Accessories program in Windows is an important time-management tool for handling desktop applications that will help you to manage your appointments, schedules, phone numbers, and many other everyday details. The Accessories tools can be minimized on your desktop so that they are available any time you are working in Windows.

• • • • • • • • • • • •

OBJECTIVES

When you complete this session, you will be able to:

- Explain the purpose and function of Windows Write.

- Access Write, enter text, and create new document files.

- Save and retrieve documents.

- Edit a document.

- Format the characters and paragraphs within a document, as well as the document itself.

- Repaginate and print documents (or print selected pages from a document).

WINDOWS WRITE

WINDOWS WRITE

CREATING DOCUMENTS WITH WRITE

PREVIEW

Windows Write is an easy-to-use word processing program. It contains basic features common to nearly all word processing programs, such as the ability to create, save, and retrieve document files; move, copy, enhance, and edit documents; set text margins and align text in various ways; and search for and replace words or phrases throughout the entire document. Although Write lacks a spell checker, a thesaurus, and other more advanced features, Write does let you create all basic documents such as letters, reports, and memos—complete with graphics, if you wish.

Starting Write and Creating Document Files

Windows Write is an accessory program located in the Accessories program group. When you start Write, you will double-click on the Accessories icon, then on the Write icon. You will see the opening Write window (shown in Figure 6.1), made up of a title bar, a menu bar, a Control-menu box, scroll bars, and a page-status area. The rest of the window is blank (similar to the opening window for Notepad), so that you can input your document.

Control-menu Box   **Menu Bar**   **Title Bar**

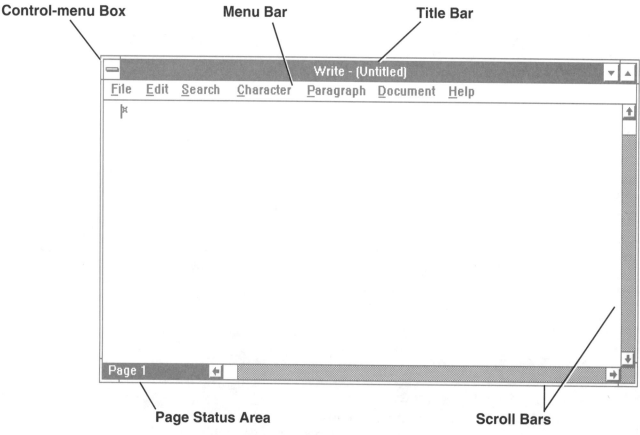

Page Status Area   **Scroll Bars**

Figure 6.1 The Write window

Note that the Write menu bar has seven pull-down menus, which are shown fully opened in Figure 6.2. Look at the options in each of these menus now, before you begin using the Write program. You will notice that you are already familiar with some of these commands because they are similar to other Windows menus and commands.

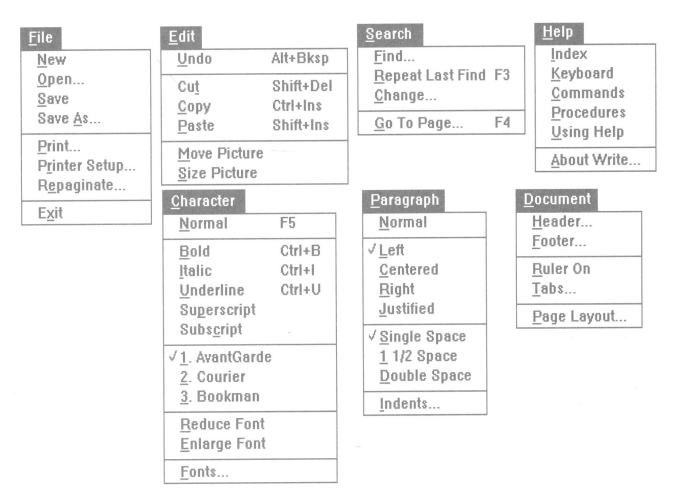

Figure 6.2 "Collage" of all seven pull-down menus:
File Edit Search Character Paragraph Document Help

When you first start using Write, the screen is clear, ready for you to start entering your text. You see Write (Untitled) in the title bar because you have not yet named the document you are about to create. You see the cursor, a thin vertical line blinking on and off at the start position. Next to the cursor you see the end marker, a starlike symbol that identifies the end of the document. When you begin keying text, the cursor will move, of course—and as it moves, it pushes the end marker along. The location of the cursor is referred to as the **insertion point** because this is where the next character you key will be inserted. Now, let's begin to use Write.

EXERCISE 6 ● 1 STARTING WRITE AND KEYING TEXT

1. Start Windows if it is not already active.

2. Start the Write program.

a. Double-click on the Accessories group window to open it if it is not already opened.

b. Double-click on the Write icon to start the Write program.

c. Click on the Maximize button to maximize the Write window.

3. Key the following text, starting at the cursor.

a. Your first and last name; then press **[Enter]**.

b. The session number and name, *Session 6, Windows Write;* then press **[Enter]**.

c. Add a few more lines of text—anything you feel like keying. Press **[Enter]** only at the end of a paragraph.

Saving and Opening a Document

Now you have text on screen, but you want to begin working on another document. You plan to return to the present document later, but first you must save it.

Selecting the Save As... command from the File menu produces the dialog box shown in Figure 6.3. The cursor appears in the Filename text

Figure 6.3

File Save As dialog box

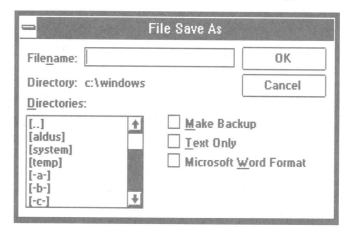

box, prompting you to key the name of your document. But first you must identify the *drive* to which you will save this document. If you want to save your document on drive A and name it PRACTICE, you would key A:PRACTICE in the text box; then click on the OK command button. Once you have an electronic record of your document, you could select the New option from the File menu to clear the screen.

But what if you selected New before you had saved the current document? Before Write clears the screen and allows you to begin a new document, it asks you whether you want to save the current document by displaying the message window shown in Figure 6.4.

Figure 6.4

(Untitled) has changed. Save Current Changes?

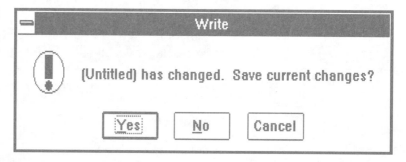

If you select "Yes," the File Save As dialog box appears, the same File Save As dialog box shown in Figure 6.3. This is Write's way of protecting you from losing text. In all cases, you use Save As... to save a document *for the first time*—to create an electronic record of your text.

Once a document is "on record," it can be retrieved by selecting the Open option on the File menu. The File Open dialog box shown in Figure 6.5 lists the available files in the current directory, including your PRACTICE file on drive A.

Figure 6.5

File Open dialog box showing PRACTICE.WRI under A:.

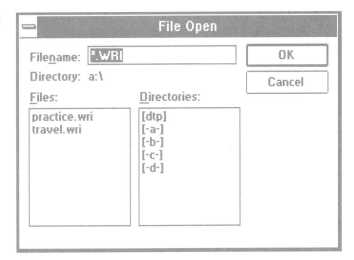

If you open the PRACTICE file and make changes, you will then want to save the new PRACTICE file, the latest version of that document. Because Write already knows the name of this file and has a record of it, you do not need to use the Save As... option. Simply use the Save option.

EXERCISE 6 . 2   SAVING AND OPENING A DOCUMENT

1. Save the practice document you created in Exercise 6.1 on your *Quick Start* disk.

    a. Select the Save As... option from the File menu.

    b. Key the filename *A:PRACTICE*, in the text box. Before the filename be sure to key the drive specification A: (or whichever letter designates the drive you are using).

    c. Click on the OK command button.

2. Create a new document using the text shown in Figure 6.6 to use as a practice document.

    a. Select the New option from the File menu.

    b. Key the text in Figure 6.6 *exactly* as it appears. As you enter copy, correct any keying errors you make by using **[Backspace]** or **[Delete]**. Do not use any Edit menu commands yet. And be sure to use an extra **[Enter]** for the extra space before the headings. Press **[Enter]** only after each heading and at the end of each paragraph.

3. Save the document using the Save As... option.

    a. Select the Save As... option from the File menu.

    b. Key the filename *A:TRVLTIPS* in the Filename text box.

    c. Click on the Make Backup check box to make a backup (that is, an extra) copy of this file—just in case.

d. Click on the OK command button.

Your document is now saved on your *Quick Start* disk. You can quit Write or begin a new document.

TRAVEL REMINDERS AND NOTES

As we enter the busiest part of our business year, the Travel Department wishes to remind all employees of our general procedures and at the same time to share some helpful travel hints.

Airline Tickets and Car Rentals

Airline reservations and car rentals must be made through the corporate Travel Department whenever possible. We suggest that you make your airline reservations as soon as you can do so; not only will you get less expensive fares, but you will also help guarantee getting a seat on the flight you want.

When you cannot make car rentals through corporate travel, we remind you that the company gets a discount from certain car rental agencies. Please see your Corporate Travel Directory for details.

Reimbursements

Except for sales representatives, all employees must use the standard Travel & Entertainment Expense Form (Form No. A22). Your monthly form must be completed, signed by your immediate supervisor, and submitted to Accounting no later than the 10th of each month for the preceding month's expenses.

Please be sure to attach receipts for all expenses over $10. This rule allows us to comply with IRS regulations.

Also, please be sure to indicate on each expense reimbursement form both (1) your department code number, (2) your personal employee ID number, and (3) your balance from the preceding month's expense report.

For reimbursement of meals with clients or potential clients, always include not only the name of each client but also his or her company affiliation and the nature of the business discussion. All entertainment expenses must be documented.

Flyers and Brochures Available

The Travel Department has a number of useful flyers and brochures for employees, including several that address safety, family vacations, and employee discounts. If you would like any of these materials or a copy of the latest Corporate Travel Directory, please call Miriam Rodriguez, Travel Department Supervisor, Extension 4445.

Figure 6.6 Sample copy for inputting document copy

VIEW 2
EDITING AND FORMATTING DOCUMENTS

PREVIEW

Editing means changing the *words* in text. Write makes it easy for you to retrieve a file you have saved and to change the text as necessary. Using Write's Edit menu (see Figure 6.2), you can easily update a report, correct sales figures, delete sentences or paragraphs, or otherwise edit documents.

    Formatting means changing the *look* or the *arrangement* of text, either of individual characters, words, or sentences, or of the entire document. The Write menu bar offers three pull-down menus for formatting text: Character, Paragraph, and Document. Before you continue, look at the options under all three menus in Figure 6.2.

Editing Text Using the Edit Menu

To delete highlighted text, you will use the Cut option on the Edit menu. To *move* highlighted text, you will use first Cut then Paste: (1) Use Cut to delete the highlighted copy, (2) position the cursor where you want to move the copy, and then (3) select Paste. The highlighted copy will now be moved to its new position.

    Similarly, to copy text, use Copy and Paste: (1) Copy the highlighted text, (2) position the cursor where you want the duplicated text to go, and (3) select Paste. The new copy will be inserted, and the original text will not be moved. Note that the Undo command is a safety feature; it allows you to cancel your last editing command. Now let's practice editing text using the Edit menu.

EXERCISE 6 • 3   ADDING, MOVING, AND CUTTING TEXT

This exercise and the following exercises use the A:TRVLTIPS document you created in View 1. If the document is not currently displayed on your screen, open the document—it has been saved on your *Quick Start* disk.

1. Indent the first word of the first paragraph under the "Reimbursements" heading.

    a. Click an insertion point immediately before the letter "E" in the word "Except."

    b. Press **[TAB]** once.

2. Change the heading "Reimbursements" to "Expense Reimbursements."

    a. Click an insertion point immediately before the letter "R" in the word "Reimbursements."

    b. Key the text *Expense* and space once.

3. Cut item "(1)" from the third paragraph in the "Expense Reimbursements" section and renumber the remaining items.

    a. Click an insertion point immediately before the word "your" in item 1.

    b. Press the mouse button and drag up to and including the right parenthesis ")" following the number "2."

c. Select the Cut option from the Edit menu. You can delete the highlighted text since you will not be moving it to another location.

d. Click an insertion point between the number "3" and the right parenthesis ")."

e. Press **[Backspace]** once to delete the number "3."

f. Key the number *2.*

4. Move the second sentence in the paragraph immediately before the "Flyers and Brochures Available" heading to the beginning of that paragraph.

   a. Click an insertion point immediately before the letter "A" in the word "All."

   b. Press the mouse button and drag across the entire sentence.

   c. Select the Cut option from the Edit menu.

   d. Click an insertion point immediately before the letter "F" in the word "For" at the beginning of the paragraph.

   e. Select the Paste option from the Edit menu.

   f. Press **[Spacebar]** twice.

Editing Text Using the Character Menu

After you highlight text, you can use the Character menu to change character attributes—that is, to change the look of text copy by selecting **bold**, *italic*, or <u>underlining</u>. (Select Normal to undo these selections.) Occasionally, you may need to use the Character menu to create subscripts and superscripts.

When you select Fonts... from the character menu, you will see the Fonts dialog box shown in Figure 6.7. Under the headings Fonts and Sizes, you simply click to indicate your choices. As you choose, your font choice will be shown in the Font Name box and your size choice in the Point Size box.

Figure 6.7

Fonts dialog box

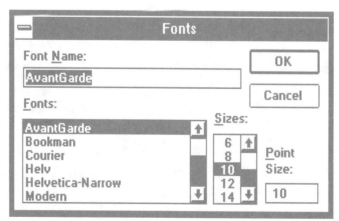

EXERCISE 6 • 4 ENHANCING TEXT

1. Italicize the first word, "All," in the paragraph above the "Flyers and Brochures Available" heading.

   a. Position the cursor directly over the word "All" and double-click. (Double-clicking on a word is like dragging across it).

b. Select the Italic option from the Character menu.

2. Change all document headings, including the title, to bold type.

   a. Click an insertion point immediately before the letter "T" in the word "TRAVEL."

   b. Press the mouse button and drag across the heading through the letter "S" in the word "NOTES."

   c. Select the Bold option from the Character menu.

   d. Repeat steps a, b, and c above to put the three side headings in bold type.

Editing Text Using the Paragraph Menu

The Paragraph menu gives you four options for formatting paragraphs: you can center paragraphs, align them at the left margin (Normal) or at the right margin, or align paragraphs at both margins (Justified). The Paragraph menu also gives you three options for line spacing: Single or Double Space, plus 1½ Space.

EXERCISE 6 • 5 FORMATTING PARAGRAPHS

1. Center the heading between the margins.

   a. Double-click on the word "TRAVEL" at the beginning of the document.

   b. Select the Centered option from the Paragraph menu.

2. At the end of the last paragraph, center the words "HAPPY TRAVEL-ING!" two lines below the last line of text.

   a. Scroll to the end of the document.

   b. Click an insertion point immediately after the period in the extension number "4445."

   c. Press **[Enter]** twice.

   d. Select the Centered option from the Paragraph menu.

   e. Press **[Caps Lock]**; then key the text *HAPPY TRAVELING!*

Editing and Formatting a Document Using the Document Menu

You will use the Document menu to create headers and footers, set tabs stops, and set margins.

A **header** is an identifying title that usually appears at the top (the "head") of the second and all subsequent pages of a document. A **footer** performs the same job but appears at the bottom of each page—again, usually beginning with the second page.

When you select Header... from the Document menu, the Header dialog box (see Figure 6.8) will display. The dialog box will be inactive, and the cursor will be positioned at the upper-left corner of the screen. Key the heading text at the cursor; then click on the appropriate buttons.

Once you have made all your selections, click on the Return to Document command button. The process is the same when you select Footer (but the dialog box labels change to Footer and Page Footer).

Figure 6.8

Header dialog box

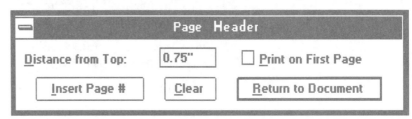

The Document menu also shows a Ruler On option. When you select this option, you will see a ruler just below the Write menu bar, as shown in Figure 6.9. (Once the Ruler On option has been selected, the menu option immediately changes to Ruler Off.)

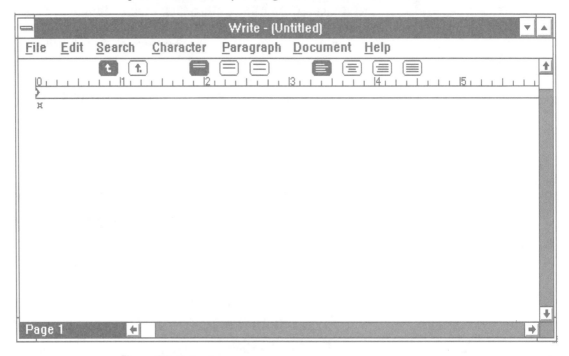

Figure 6.9 Ruler line

The ruler offers several features besides ruler numbers. Above the ruler are three sets of symbols:

a. The first set, the two small arrows, allows you to change normal tab alignment (Write's default) to decimal tab alignment, used to align decimal numbers on the period—a great convenience when entering dollar amounts. Decimal tabs will be discussed later.

b. The next set shows three miniature screens with lines representing Single Space, 1½ Space, and Double Space.

c. The third set shows four miniature screens representing left alignment, centered alignment, right alignment, and full alignment at both left and right margins (called **full justification**).

The Document menu also lets you set tab stops. Write has preset tabs every half inch along a text line. To change tab settings, select Tabs... and you will see the Tabs dialog box, shown in Figure 6.10. Enter numbers in the Positions boxes to set the new tab stops. To align a column of decimal numbers on the period, select the Decimal option by placing an X in the Decimal box. The OK, Cancel, and Clear All buttons allow you to change or approve your selections.

Figure 6.10

Tabs dialog box

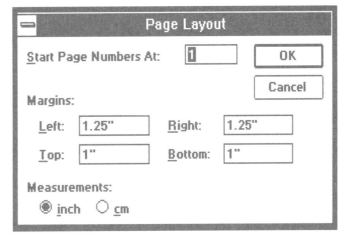

Write has preset left and right margins of 1¼ inches and top and bottom margins of 1 inch. To change margins, select Page Layout... on the Document menu and use the Page Layout dialog box, shown in Figure 6.11, to enter the new margin values. Also, if your document does not start with page 1, enter the correct starting page number in the Start Page Numbers At box.

Figure 6.11

Page Layout dialog box with default values

EXERCISE 6 ● 6   FORMATTING A DOCUMENT

1. Change the left and right margins to 1 inch on each side.

   a. Select the Page Layout... option from the Document menu.

   b. Press **[Tab]** to highlight the Left text box.

   c. Key the number *1*.

   d. Press **[Tab]** to highlight the Right text box and key the number *1*.

   e. Click on the OK command button.

2. Change the line spacing to double spacing.

   a. Click an insertion point immediately before the letter "T" in the document heading.

b. Press the mouse button and drag to the end of the document. The entire document should be selected (highlighted).

c. Select the Double Space option from the Paragraph menu.

3. Add a Footer—"Travel Tips"—and a page number only for the second page.

a. Select the Footer... option from the Document menu.

b. Select the Right option from the Paragraph menu. Do not check the Print on First Page box because you do not want the footer on page 1.

c. Key the footer text *Travel Tips - page* and space once.

d. Click on the Insert Page # command button in the Page Footer dialog box.

e. Click on the Return to Document command button.

Using Search Options

Flipping through pages of even a short document in an effort to find a word or phrase can be time-consuming and frustrating. Write simplifies such searches.

Look at the Search menu options shown in Figure 6.2. The first option, Find..., helps you locate a word or phrase, and Repeat Last Find looks for the next occurrence, if any, of that same word or phrase. A Find dialog box (similar to the Change dialog box discussed next and shown below) will prompt you to enter the word or phrase you are searching for.

Selecting the Change... option brings a Change dialog box on screen. Shown in Figure 6.12, this box prompts you to enter two key pieces of information: Find What and Change To.

Figure 6.12

Change dialog box

Change
Find What: IRS
Change To: Internal Revenue Service
☐ Whole Word   ☒ Match Upper/Lowercase
Find Next	Change, then Find	Change	Change All

EXERCISE 6 • 7   SEARCHING AND REPLACING

1. Change the letters "IRS" to "Internal Revenue Service."

a. Select the Change... option from the Search menu.

b. Key the letters *IRS* in the Find What text box; then press **[Tab]**.

c. Key the words *Internal Revenue Service* in the Change To text box.

d. Click in the Match Upper/Lowercase check box to select it. You want to check this box because you want to find only the uppercase (capital) letters that match the search.

e. Click on the Find Next command button. Write will search the text and stop and highlight the search word when it is found.

f. Click on the Change command button when the search word is located.

g. Click on the Find Next command button. Since a match cannot be found, a message box will appear indicating that the search is complete.

h. Click on the OK command button on the message box.

i. Double-click on the Control-menu box to close the Change window.

2. Change the word "flyers" to "fliers" (there are two occurrences).

a. Select the Change... option from the Search menu.

b. Key the word *flyers* in the Find What text box.

c. Key the word *fliers* in the Change To text box.

d. Click on the Match Upper/Lowercase check box to deselect it.

e. Click on the Find Next command button.

f. Click on the Change command button when the search word is located in the text.

g. Continue the search by repeating steps e and f until the Search Complete message box displays.

h. Click on the OK command button on the message box; then double-click on the Change dialog box to close the window.

3. Save your revised TRVLTIPS file once again.

VIEW 3
REPAGINATING AND PRINTING DOCUMENTS

PREVIEW

The purpose of creating documents is almost always to print them. But editing and formatting alone do not ensure that your document will print exactly as you wish. Before you print, therefore, Write allows you to view the document page by page on screen. If you want to change the page breaks, you can use the Repaginate option on Write's File menu. The Repaginate... option and the Print... option are used hand in hand.

Repaginating Documents

To see page breaks on screen *before* printing, you will pull down the File menu and select Repaginate.... The Repaginate Document dialog box has only one choice: Confirm Page Breaks. When you select this option, another dialog box appears, the Repaginating Document box shown in Figure 6.13. While this box is on screen, Write will show you how it plans to break pages in your document. You approve each page break by pressing

Figure 6.13

Repaginating Document dialog box

the Confirm button, and you use the up or the down button to suggest different page breaks.

Printing Your Document

To print a document, you will pull down the File menu and select Print....
The Print dialog box will appear as shown in Figure 6.14. After Copies,

Figure 6.14

Print dialog box

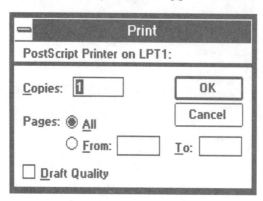

you will enter the number of copies of the document you want to print. After Pages, you will select All if you want to print the entire document; if not, you will select the option below All, and then fill in the range of pages you want to print by entering the appropriate page numbers after From and To.

EXERCISE 6 . 8   REPAGINATING AND PRINTING A DOCUMENT

To practice repaginating and printing a document, in this exercise you will use the TRVLTIPS file saved on your *Quick Start* disk. Open this file before you proceed.

1. Check the document page breaks.

   a. Select the Repaginate... option from the File menu.

   b. Click on the Confirm Page Breaks check box to select it; then click on the OK command button. (You want Write to stop at each page break and display it on the screen before proceeding.) A small arrow will appear in the left margin indicating the suggested page break.

   c. Click on the Up command button to move the page break up one line. Notice the line becomes highlighted.

   d. Click on the Down command button to move the page break down one line; then confirm the page break by clicking on the Confirm button.

2. Save your document.

3. Print one copy of the document.

   a. Select the Print... option from the File menu.

   b. Click on the OK command button.

4. Exit the Write program.

Let's assume you've just learned that Miriam Rodriquez left the company. You need to retrieve the document, make the name correction, and print a revised copy of TRVLTIPS.

5. Open the TRVLTIPS file and change "Miriam Rodriquez" to "Shellee Winston."

   a. Start the Write program and open the TRVLTIPS document file.

   b. Select the Change... option from the Search menu.

   c. Key the name *Miriam Rodriquez* in the Find What text box; then press **[Tab]**.

   d. Enter the name *Shellee Winston* in the Change To text box; then click on the Find Next command button. When the next occurrence is found, click on the change button.

   e. Click on the Find Next command button. The Search Complete message box appears.

   f. Click on the OK command button to close the Search Complete message box.

   g. Double-click on the Control-menu box to close the Find dialog box.

6. Save your file.

7. Print one copy of the revised document.

   a. Select the Print... option from the File menu.

   b. Click on the OK command button.

8. Exit the Write program and exit Windows.

SUMMARY

Windows Write offers all the basic tools you will need to create documents, edit the copy to make changes and corrections, format the text so that it is visually attractive, paginate the document, and finally print all or part of the document. Perhaps best of all, Write lets you save that document for future use. The more you practice using Write, the more familiar and comfortable you will be using it.

OBJECTIVES

When you complete this session, you will be able to:

- Explain the purpose and function of Windows Paintbrush.

- Access Paintbrush and use its electronic tools to create graphic files.

- Save, retrieve, and print graphic files.

- Use the draw feature to create images.

- Color, insert, cut, copy, and move text and drawings.

- Edit graphic files.

WINDOWS PAINTBRUSH

VIEWS
Working with Paintbrush
Creating, Saving, and Printing Drawings

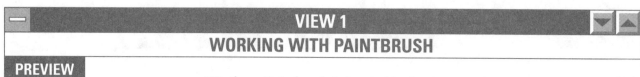

WINDOWS PAINTBRUSH

Windows Paintbrush provides tools for drawing simple to complex images—or **graphics**, as they are called. Paintbrush has features that make it easy to produce attractive artwork that can be used as stand-alone images or placed in newsletters, posters, letterheads, advertisements, and other documents. In this session, you will use Paintbrush tools to create, save, and print your drawings. As you work with Paintbrush, you may sometimes find it a bit puzzling at first, but stick with it. After a while, the results will be rewarding.

VIEW 1
WORKING WITH PAINTBRUSH

PREVIEW

Figure 7.1

Paintbrush icon

Windows Paintbrush is located in the Accessories program group. When you start Paintbrush, you double-click on the Paintbrush icon, which resembles a painter's palette (see Figure 7.1). Like other windows you have seen, the Paintbrush window contains a Control-menu box, a title bar, minimize and maximize buttons, scroll bars, a work (or drawing) area, and, of course, a menu bar (see Figure 7.2). But the Paintbrush window also has three unique tool areas: a toolbox, a line-width box, and a color and shades palette. Before we discuss these tool areas, let's talk about electronic painting and drawing and how the Paintbrush program works.

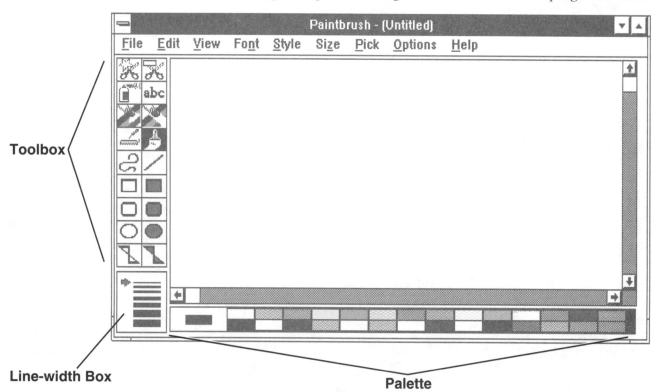

Figure 7.2 Paintbrush window

The Paintbrush Tools

The drawing area of the Paintbrush window is where all the action takes place. The tools you need are to the left of the drawing area and beneath it, as shown in Figure 7.2. To draw or paint, you must first select (that is, click on) a tool from the toolbox (see Figure 7.3); then move the pointer to the drawing area, where it becomes an icon of the tool you selected.

Figure 7.3

Paintbrush toolbox

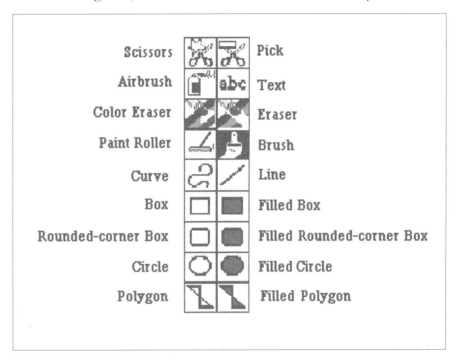

Scissors			Pick
Airbrush			Text
Color Eraser			Eraser
Paint Roller			Brush
Curve			Line
Box			Filled Box
Rounded-corner Box			Filled Rounded-corner Box
Circle			Filled Circle
Polygon			Filled Polygon

The procedures for using each tool differ slightly. To help you prepare for completing the exercises in this session, let's look at two basic methods of using the tools in Paintbrush:

1. When using one of the graphic or painting tools, click on the mouse, drag the tool's image to where you want it, and then release the mouse. A line, box, circle, or whatever other shape you drew appears in the exact size and location you indicated. Now draw additional shapes. You determine the line thickness before you begin to draw by selecting from the line-width box. Similarly, you determine color, shade, or pattern for closed objects in your drawing by selecting from the Palette.

2. Inserting text in a drawing is similar to using a word processing program. Select the text tool, click an insertion point, and then key the text. The text can be moved around the screen easily—it can even be placed inside a graphic, if you like.

There are many tools and menu options available to you to enhance your drawing. For example, you can color and shade lines; insert, cut, copy, and move text; and change the type attributes. You can even tilt, flip, stretch, and shrink all or portions of your drawing!

The tools in the Paintbrush toolbox (Figure 7.3) can be classified into four groups: *graphic tools*, *painting tools*, *modifying tools*, and a *text tool*. In View 1, you will work with the first two tools; in View 2, the remaining tools.

Using Graphic Tools

Paintbrush has ten graphic tools: two line tools for curved and straight lines and eight shape tools for drawing objects. Use the Curve and Line tools to draw lines. Before you draw the line, select the width you want from the line-width box.

The Box (filled and unfilled) and Rounded-corner Box (filled and unfilled) tools are used to draw boxes and rectangles with square or rounded corners. If you want a perfectly square box, hold down **[Shift]** as you draw the box. Before you draw the box, determine the width of the border by making a selection from the Line-width box, and determine the shade, pattern, or color of a filled box by making a selection from the Palette.

The Circle (filled and unfilled) tools are used to draw circles and ovals. Hold down **[Shift]** as you draw the circle if you want a perfect circle; otherwise, you may get an oval. Before you draw the circle, select the border width from the Line-width box, and select the fill (if any) from the Palette.

The Polygon (filled and unfilled) tools are used to draw multisided objects with straight sides. Before you draw the object, select the border width from the Line-width box, and select the fill (if any) from the Palette.

Before you look at the painting tools, you will have a chance to put the graphic tools to work by creating the sample drawing illustrated in Figure 7.4. Because artistic ability varies from one person to another, your graphic may differ slightly from the illustrations in the Paintbrush exercises. Don't worry—just do your best and have fun!

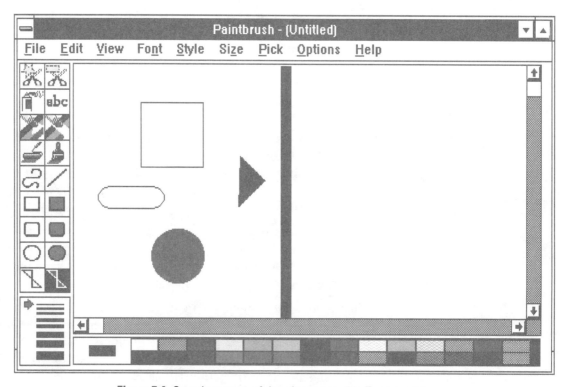

Figure 7.4 Sample screen of drawing created in Exercise 7.1

EXERCISE 7 • 1   USING THE GRAPHIC TOOLS

1. Start Windows if it is not already active.

2. Start the Paintbrush program:

   a. Double-click on the Accessories group window to open it if it is not already opened.

   b. Double-click on the Paintbrush icon to start the Paintbrush program.

   c. Click on the maximize button to maximize the Paintbrush window.

3. Draw a thick vertical line down the center of the page (see Figure 7.4):

   a. Select the Line tool from the toolbox.

   b. Select the thickest (the last) line from the Line-width box.

   c. Position the Line icon in the drawing area (**not on the Menu bar**) approximately between the Pick and the Options menu names (see Figure 7.4).

   d. Press and hold down **[Shift]**, press and hold down the mouse button, and then drag to the bottom of the drawing area. Release the mouse; then release **[Shift]** when you reach the bottom of the screen. (You hold down **[Shift]** to make sure you have an absolutely straight line. You release the mouse **before** you release **[Shift]** to insure that the line remains straight.)

NOTE: If you make an error or if you click or release the mouse button before you intend to, select the Undo option from the Edit menu. Undo cancels all the work you've done up to the point at which you selected the tool you are currently using.

4. In the upper half of the left side of the page, draw a perfect square box with a thin border (see Figure 7.4):

   a. Select the unfilled Square Box tool.

   b. Select the thinnest (the topmost) line from the Line-width box.

   c. Position the Box icon in the upper portion of the drawing area (**not on the menu bar**) approximately between the Font and Style menu names (see Figure 7.4).

   d. Press and hold down **[Shift]**, press and hold down the mouse button, and then drag down and to the right until you have a box similar to the one in Figure 7.4. Release the mouse; then release **[Shift]** when you have the desired box size.

5. Draw a perfect filled circle in the lower half of the left side of the page (see Figure 7.4):

   a. Select the Filled Circle tool.

   b. Select from the Palette the color of your choice (if you have a color monitor) or the pattern of your choice (if you have a monochrome monitor).

c. Position the Filled Circle tool icon in the lower portion of the drawing area (**not on the menu bar**) between the Font and Style menu names.

d. Press and hold down **[Shift]**, press and hold down the mouse button, and then drag down and to the right until you have a circle similar to the one in Figure 7.4. Release the mouse; then release **[Shift]** when you have the desired box size.

6. Experiment with the other graphic tools by drawing one or two filled or unfilled objects on the left side of the drawing area. Do not draw anything on the right side.

Using Painting Tools

Unlike graphic tools, painting tools are not constrained. You can use the painting tools to draw freeform objects and fill graphic objects.

There are three painting tools (see Figure 7.3)—Airbrush, Paint Roller, and Brush. Like a can of spray paint, the Airbrush tool sprays a light circular pattern of colored dots, instead of painting a solid color. Click once on the mouse button to get one "spurt" of color; hold down the mouse button and drag to get a trail of spray color.

The Paint Roller tool fills a shape with color or shading. The shape must be completely enclosed (like a box or a circle); it cannot have an opening, or the paint will spill out onto the area around the shape. The Paint Roller icon looks like a paint roller spreading paint.

The Brush tool paints a solid stroke of color the width of the line selected in the Line-width box. The shape of the brush can be changed, as you will see later.

In order to use these painting tools properly, you must understand the purpose and function of the Paintbrush Palette.

The Paintbrush Palette

The Palette offers two choices: a **foreground color** and a **background color**. The foreground color is the color you get when you draw with the graphic tools or paint with one of the painting tools. The foreground color is also the fill color that goes inside filled shapes (boxes, circles, and so on). The background color is the color of the border around the edges of filled shapes, as well as the background color of your screen whenever you start a new Paintbrush file.

Colors and patterns can be changed easily: (1) to change the foreground color or pattern, point on the desired color or pattern and click the *left* mouse button; (2) to change the background color or pattern, point on the desired color or pattern and click the *right* mouse button. Now practice using these painting tools on the right side of the drawing area, as illustrated in Figure 7.5.

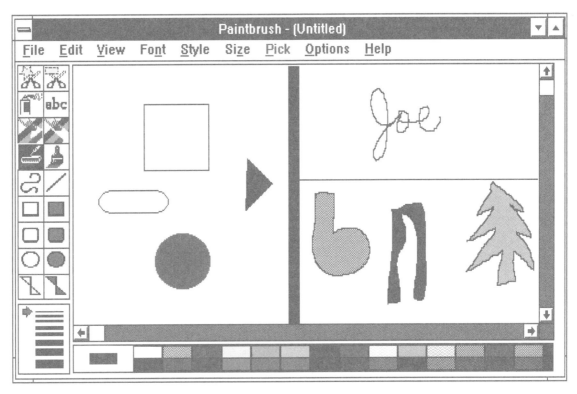

Figure 7.5 Sample screen showing completed Exercise 7.2

EXERCISE 7 . 2   USING THE PAINTING TOOLS

1. Draw a thin horizontal line at the center of the right-hand side of the page (see Figure 7.5):

   a. Select the Line tool from the toolbox.

   b. Select a thin line from the Line-width box.

   c. Position the Line icon about halfway down the right-hand side of the drawing area, press and hold down **[Shift]**, and then drag a line across the page.

2. With the Brush tool, write your first name in the upper portion of the right side of the drawing area (see Figure 7.5):

   a. Select the Brush tool.

   b. Select a foreground (fill) color (or pattern) of your choice by pointing on your selection on the Palette and clicking the left mouse button.

   c. Position the Brush tool icon (a dot) at the starting point, press the mouse button, and "write" your name.

3. With the Brush tool, draw three different closed shapes in the lower portion of the right side of the drawing area (see Figure 7.5):

  a. Select the Brush tool, if it is not already selected.

  b. Select a background color (or pattern) of your choice by pointing on your selection on the Palette and clicking the right mouse button.

  c. Draw the shape. Be sure you make a closed shape.

  d. Follow steps *a* through *c* above until you have created three objects. Remember, you can select the Undo option from File menu to delete unwanted objects, but it will delete everything that you did since selecting the current tool.

4. Use the Paint Roller to fill the interior of two of the objects you created in step 3 above with a different color or pattern:

  a. Select the Paint Roller tool from the toolbox.

  b. Select the foreground color or pattern from the Palette by clicking on the color or pattern of your choice with the left mouse button.

  c. Position the pointed tip of the Paint Roller tool icon inside the object you want to fill.

  d. Click the left mouse button.

  e. Fill one more object by following steps *b* through *d* above.

5. Use the Airbrush to fill the interior of the last of your three objects with a different color or pattern:

  a. Select the Airbrush tool from the toolbox.

  b. Select the foreground color or pattern from the Palette by clicking on the color or pattern of your choice with the left mouse button.

  c. Position the Airbrush tool icon inside the object where you want the airbrush stroke, press and hold the mouse button, and "spray" the interior of the object.

Normally, you save and print your graphic, but since this was a learning exercise, clear the screen and exit Paintbrush.

6. Exit the Paintbrush program:

  a. Select the Exit option from the File menu. A warning dialog box will be displayed indicating that you have not saved the current document.

  b. Click on the No command button to clear the screen and exit the Paintbrush program.

PREVIEW

Even if you have steady hands and a good imagination, you may need or want to modify your work. To do so, Paintbrush provides a number of modify tools and menu options. And while a picture will often be all you need to express your thought, feeling, or mood, you will sometimes want to include text in your graphics. Paintbrush offers you a great variety of type fonts and sizes. Finally, of course, you will want to print your work. Here, again, Paintbrush offers great flexibility; you may print all or only part of a drawing, as you wish.

Modifying a Drawing

You can use several techniques to modify drawings. You have already learned one of the easiest—the Undo command. But that command will only erase work in progress (work done since you last selected a tool). Also, the Undo command is not selective; that is, it forces you to erase everything you have done. To overcome these problems, Paintbrush has four modifying tools—Scissors, Pick, Eraser, and Color Eraser. Let's look at how you would use each one before beginning the actual exercises.

Scissors and Pick Tools. The Scissors and the Pick tools resemble one another. Their icons hint at the subtle difference in their functions. Because the Scissors is used to select irregularly shaped portions of a drawing, the icon shows a pair of scissors cutting an irregular shape. Because the Pick tool is used to select rectangular areas, its icon shows a pair of scissors cutting a rectangular shape.

To select a shape with the Pick tool, position the cursor just above and to the left of the object to be selected, press the left mouse button and drag the cursor down and to the right until the dotted line completely encloses the desired selection, and then click the right button. Be sure that the entire object is within the dotted rectangle that is displayed. Only the area within the dotted rectangle can be modified.

To select a shape with the Scissors tool, position the cursor near the object to be selected, press the left mouse button, and drag an irregular line around the shape to be selected. Since you control the form the line takes, you can enclose as much or as little within the dotted rectangle as needed.

Once you have selected an area, you can use the options on the Edit and Pick menus to modify the area in several ways. The Edit menu options are Cut, Copy, and Paste. The Pick menu options are Flip Horizontal, Flip Vertical, Inverse, Shrink & Grow, and Tilt.

Erasers. Paintbrush has two erasers—one that erases anything in its path and a color eraser that erases only a selected color. To change the selected foreground color to the selected background color over a selected area, drag the color eraser over the area. To change all of the selected foreground color to the selected background color, double-click on the color eraser.

Now you will use these tools to create an image similar to the one illustrated in Figure 7.6.

Figure 7.6

Sample screen showing completed Exercise 7.3

EXERCISE 7 . 3   USING THE MODIFYING TOOLS

1. Start Paintbrush if it is not already running. Open the CHESS.BMP file in the WINDOWS subdirectory:

   a. Select the Open... option from the File menu.

   b. Verify that the BMP button is selected.

   c. Select the CHESS.BMP file displayed in the directory listing.

2. Copy the yellow chess piece in the drawing to the Clipboard: (If your monitor does not display color, select the chess piece shown on the left side of the opened window.)

   a. Select the Scissors tool (the one on the left).

   b. Place the Scissors icon above and to the left of the chess piece to be cut.

   c. Press the mouse button and draw a freeform line around the graphic, as shown in Figure 7.7.

   d. Select the Copy option from the Edit menu. The chess piece will be copied to the clipboard.

3. Close the CHESS.BMP file—**do not save the changes**:

   a. Select the New option from the File menu.

   b. Respond No to the message box "Save Current Image CHESS.BMP?" by clicking on the No command button.

4. Paste the chess piece into the new document:
   Select the Paste option from the Edit menu. The cut chess piece will be pasted on the page.

5. Remove the black color from the object:

   a. Select white as the background color (click on white with the right mouse button).

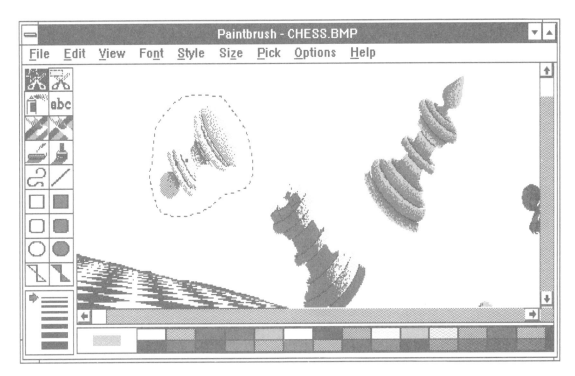

Figure 7.7 Screen showing freeform cut line around yellow chess piece

b. Select black as the foreground color (click on black with the left mouse button).

c. Double-click on the color eraser (the one on the left). All black color should be erased.

6. Flip the object vertically:

a. Select the Pick tool, click above and to the left of the object, drag a dotted line down and to the right, and then release the mouse button. Make sure the entire chess piece is enclosed in the box.

b. Select the Flip Vertical option from the Pick menu.

7. Add an unfilled, black-border rectangle around the graphic, as shown in Figure 7.6:

a. Click on the color black on the Palette. Next, select the unfilled Box tool. Select a thin line.

b. Drag a box around the graphic. Remember, if you misplace the graphic, select the Undo option from the File menu.

Adding Text to a Drawing

The Text tool is shown as an **abc** icon in the toolbox (see Figure 7.3). When the Text tool is selected, the pointer changes to the I-beam cursor shape used by Write and Notepad. To use the Text took, click an insertion point where you want the text to begin, and key the text. Since you cannot change the font, style, or size after the text has been keyed, make these selections after you select the Text tool and before you click an insertion point.

Changing the Type Specifications

The appearance of the type you use in your Paintbrush drawings consists of four elements: font, style, size, and color. Except for color, the rest of these elements have many variations, as shown in the menus illustrated in Figure 7.8.

Fo**n**t
√ **Terminal**
Helv
Courier
Tms Rmn
Symbol
Roman
Script
Modern
Small Fonts
ZapfDingbats
System

St**y**le	
√ **Normal**	
Bold	Ctrl+B
Italic	Ctrl+I
Underline	Ctrl+U
Outline	
Shadow	

Si**z**e			
6	24	44	66
√ 8 *	26	45	70
10	28	48	72
12	30	50	74
15	**32**	52	75
16	36	54	76
18	37	56	78
19	38	57	80
20	**40**	60	84
22	42	64	

Figure 7.8 Font, Style, and Size menus

A **font** is the actual design or shape shared by an entire alphabet of characters. You select the desired font from those available on the Font menu (three common font names are Courier, Times Roman, and Helvetica). All fonts have several variations or styles—bold, italic, outline, and more. Use the Style menu to select a desired style.

Type is measured in **points**, the printer's unit of measure. You don't need to memorize a new measurement system; just remember there are 72 points in 1 inch. Only certain sizes are available for each font or style. Select font and style first, and then the sizes available for those selections will display on the Size menu with an asterisk.

EXERCISE 7 • 4   WORKING WITH TEXT

Continue the work you began in Exercise 7.3.

1. To the right of the graphic, place the text "Chess is fun!" in 36-point Times Roman (see Figure 7.6):

   a. Select the Text tool from the toolbox.

   b. Select the Times Roman (Tms Rmn) font from the Font menu.

   c. Select 36 from the Size menu.

   d. Click an insertion point where you wish the text to begin, and then key the word *Chess* and press **[Enter]**.

   e. Key the remainder of the text, *is fun!*

2. Adjust the position of the text, if necessary:

   a. Select the Pick tool from the toolbox.

b. Draw a dotted box around the text.

c. Point inside the box; then press and hold the mouse button while dragging the text to the desired spot.

3. Place a light blue (color monitor) or a simple pattern (monochrome monitor) background inside the box:

a. Select the Paint Roller tool from the toolbox.

b. Select the lightest blue (or pattern).

c. Point inside the rectangle, but not directly on any of the lines or objects, and then click the mouse button.

d. Point inside the enclosed portion of the letter "e"; then click the mouse button.

4. Save a copy of your work:

a. Select the Save As... option from the File menu.

b. Key the filename *A:Graphic* in the text box.

c. Verify that the BMP button is selected.

d. Click on the OK command button. Be patient after you issue this command because it takes a long time to save one of these files.

Printing a Drawing

Paintbrush provides several options for printing your drawings. You can print: (1) the whole drawing or just a portion of it, (2) a final copy or a rough draft, (3) one copy or multiple copies, and (4) actual, reduced, or enlarged size. These choices are made in the Print dialog box (see Figure 7.9).

Figure 7.9

Print dialog box

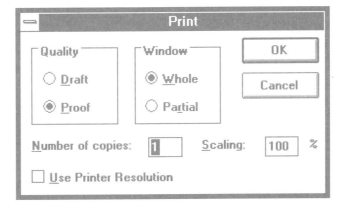

Draft quality has lighter, less-defined letters and takes less time to print than Proof quality output. If you wish to print only a portion of your drawing, use the Pick tool to select the part you want to print, and then click on the Partial button in the Window box. If you want more than one copy, indicate how many in the Number of copies text box. Use the Scaling text box to indicate the size of your printed copy: the number 100 for actual size (that is, 100%); a number smaller than 100 (for example, 50, for 50%) if you want to reduce the printed copy; or a number greater than 100 (for example, 125, for 125%) to enlarge the printed copy.

EXERCISE 7 • 5   PRINTING A DRAWING

1. Print a draft copy of your drawing:

    a. Select the Print... option from the File menu. The Print dialog box (Figure 7.9) is displayed.

    b. Click on the Draft button.

    c. Verify that the Whole button is selected in the Window box.

    d. Verify Number of copies is 1 and Scaling is 100%.

    e. Click on the OK command button.

Inspect your printed drawing. Remember, this is *draft quality*, so it may not be very sharp and clear. After you see a printed copy, make any adjustments to your drawing that are needed.

2. Print a 75% proof copy of your drawing:

    a. Select the Print... option from the File menu.

    b. Click on the Proof button if it is not already selected.

    c. Verify that the Whole button is selected in the Window box.

    d. Verify Number of copies is 1.

    e. Drag across or double-click on the scaling text box to select the number; then key the number *75*.

    f. Click on the "Use Printer Resolution" check box to select it. This will produce a much better quality output.

    g. Click on the OK command button.

3. Exit the Paintbrush program and close Windows:

    a. Select the Exit option from the File menu.

    b. If prompted, save the current document (A:Graphic).

    c. Double-click on the Control-menu box to close the Program Manager.

    d. Exit Windows.

SUMMARY

Windows Paintbrush provides tools for drawing simple to complex graphics. Paintbrush is located in the Accessories program group. The drawing area of the Paintbrush window is where all the action takes place. The Paintbrush toolbox provides many tools and menu options to enhance your drawing. You can color and shade lines, insert, cut, copy and move text, and enhance your drawings in many other ways. Also,

Paintbrush supplies you with painting tools to allow for drawing of freeform objects and to fill in objects with color or shading. The Palette is another enhancement to the Paintbrush program, which offers choices to place color in the foreground or background of your drawing.

Producing newsletters, reports, letters and memos with text in varying sizes and typefaces is nice, but it is not enough today—not when you have the tools available to you like those provided in Windows Paintbrush. Paintbrush is the answer to livening up documents to capture the attention of your reader.

• • • • • • • • • • • • • •

OBJECTIVES

When you complete this session, you will be able to:

- Explain the use of the Windows Control Panel.
- Define the available Control Panel options.
- Change the Windows color scheme.
- Change the desktop pattern and the desktop wallpaper.
- Assign and reassign printers and printer status.

SESSION 8

THE CONTROL PANEL

VIEWS
Working with the Control Panel
Changing Printer Settings

THE CONTROL PANEL

As you now realize, Windows provides a desktop environment complete with sound, color, and a mouse—an environment you can change as you wish by using the Control Panel. Windows Control Panel provides a quick and easy way to modify or customize both the desktop environment and several of your system's original hardware and software settings—that is, your system's defaults. And Windows implements Control Panel changes immediately, without requiring you to reboot (shut your computer down and start it up again), unlike most other software programs.

VIEW 1
WORKING WITH THE CONTROL PANEL

PREVIEW

Assume you want to change the system defaults that determine the screen color or that turn off the sound of an annoying warning beep. Your first step is to start the Control Panel by double-clicking on the Control Panel icon, a program item icon within the Main group window. A Control Panel window will open, similar to the one shown in Figure 8.1.

Figure 8.1

Control Panel window

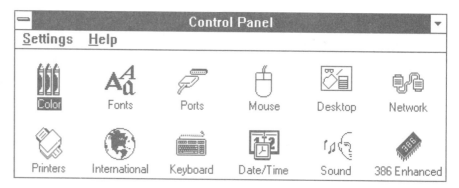

EXERCISE 8 . 1   STARTING THE CONTROL PANEL

1. Double-click on the Main window in the Program Manager.

2. Double-click on the Control Panel icon to display the Control Panel window.

The Control Panel Window

The Control Panel window displays 10 to 12 icons, depending on your computer system hardware. Each icon represents a tool you can use to set or alter hardware default settings. All 12 icons are illustrated in Figures 8.2 through 8.13, and their functions are described below:

Figure 8.2

Color icon

Color Icon. Changes the color scheme of your desktop workspace, including borders, title bars, and background colors. See Figure 8.2.

Figure 8.3 Fonts icon	Fonts	**Fonts Icon.** Permits you to add or remove fonts for your screen and printer. See Figure 8.3.
Figure 8.4 Ports icon	Ports	**Ports Icon.** Lets you attach printers and other communicating devices to your computer. See Figure 8.4.
Figure 8.5 Mouse icon	Mouse	**Mouse Icon.** Changes the speed and the way your mouse performs. See Figure 8.5.
Figure 8.6 Desktop icon	Desktop	**Desktop Icon.** Changes the appearance of the background of your Windows display by allowing you to change the patterns or pictures used in it. See Figure 8.6.
Figure 8.7 Printers icon	Printers	**Printers Icon.** Lets you add or remove a printer or change the way the printer is set up for you to use with Windows. See Figure 8.7.
Figure 8.8 International icon	International	**International Icon.** Allows you to change certain settings to represent another country, specifies language or keyboard to use, selects either the metric or the English system of measurement, offers number formats, specifies dates, and specifies time and currency formats. See Figure 8.8.
Figure 8.9 Keyboard icon	Keyboard	**Keyboard Icon.** Adjusts the time setting for repeating keystrokes when keys are held down. See Figure 8.9.
Figure 8.10 Date and Time icon	Date/Time	**Date/Time Icon.** Enables you to correct the date and time displayed by the system. See Figure 8.10.
Figure 8.11 Sound icon	Sound	**Sound Icon.** Turns on and off the beep you hear when the computer senses an error. See Figure 8.11.
Figure 8.12 Network icon	Network	**Network Icon.** Lets you control how Windows works when it is installed on a network. This icon will only appear if Windows is told it is being used on a network. See Figure 8.12.
Figure 8.13 386 Enhanced icon	386 Enhanced	**386 Enhanced Icon.** Allows you to adjust how programs work with Windows in an Enhanced mode, that is, if you are running Windows on an Intel® 80386-based computer. This icon will only appear if Windows itself is operating in the Enhanced 386 mode.

Also in the Control Panel window are two menus: (1) a Settings menu, which activates each of the Control Panel options shown in Figure 8.1

(this menu is not needed if you are using a mouse), and (2) a Help menu, which provides assistance for every Control Panel option.

Changing Windows' Color Scheme

One of the first things you notice about the Windows environment is how it uses colors (if you have a color monitor) or shades (if you have a monochrome monitor) in window elements and dialog boxes. Up to now, you have "accepted" the color scheme as it appeared on your screen; however, you can change the color scheme by using the Color option to (1) select from a set of predefined schemes or (2) create your own scheme.

    To change the color scheme, double-click on the Color icon. The Color dialog box (shown in Figure 8.14) is displayed, and in the center of this box is a sample window. Each of the elements (window text, active border, etc.) is displayed in its selected color. The various colors in the Color window make up its **color scheme**. The name of the current color scheme is highlighted in the Color Schemes drop-down list box. For example, the color scheme used in Figure 8.14 is called *Quick Start.*

Figure 8.14

Color dialog box

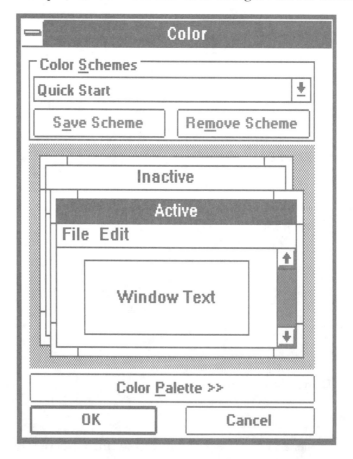

    Using a Predefined Color Scheme. To view the list of predefined color schemes, click on the drop-down arrow of the Color Schemes drop-down list box. If you select one of the listed schemes, you can preview the results in the sample window.

EXERCISE 8 . 2 USING A PREDEFINED WINDOWS COLOR SCHEME

1. Double-click on the Color icon.

2. Make a note of the selected color scheme.

3. Click on the scroll arrow in the Color Scheme drop-down list box; then click on the Arizona color scheme.

4. View the results of the new selection. Then repeat step 3 above and select another color scheme.

5. Reset the color scheme to the default—the original setting in step 2 above.

6. Click on the Cancel button when you leave the Color program so you do not permanently change your computer's color scheme.

Creating a New Color Scheme. In addition to selecting from predefined color schemes, you can use the color palette to add colors and to "custom mix" colors. To access the color palette, select the Color Palette >> command button. Two palettes will be added to the right side of the screen—Basic Colors and Custom Colors (Figure 8.15).

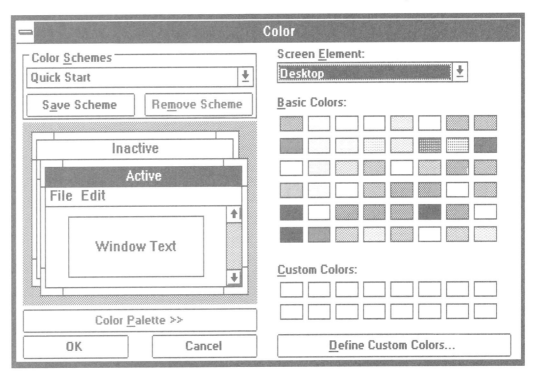

Figure 8.15 Color Palette

Changing colors is a two-step process: (1) select the window element whose color you want to change; then (2) select a color. The simplest way to select a window element is to click on the elements in the sample window. If you know the element's name, you can select the element from the drop-down list box in the upper-right corner of the window.

After you "color" your window elements, click on the OK command button to implement you color scheme. When the Basic Colors palette doesn't have the color you want, you can use the Custom Colors palette. Mixing custom colors is an advanced feature and is not covered in *Quick Start*.

EXERCISE 8 . 3   CREATING A WINDOWS COLOR SCHEME

This exercise assumes that you have a color monitor. If you have a monochrome monitor, select a shade or pattern in place of a color.

1. If it is not ready running, double-click on the Control Panel icon to open the application.

2. Double-click on the Color icon; then click on the Color Palette >> command button to display the color palette (Figure 8.15).

3. Select the Active Title Bar (it appears as a choice in the box immediately below the words "Screen Element").

4. Click on the color of your choice. Notice the element you selected is now the new color.

5. Select the Inactive Title Bar.

6. Click on a second color of your choice.

7. Continue selecting screen elements and colors until you have a pleasing color combination.

8. Click on the Cancel button when you leave the Color dialog box. You will be returned to the Control Panel window.

Customizing the Desktop

In addition to changing the color scheme of the window elements, you can also change the appearance of the desktop (the background area of the Program Manager and the minimized icons). For your desktop you can select (1) a color from the Color dialog box, (2) a pattern (such as the one shown in Figure 8.16) from the Desktop dialog box, or (3) a drawing from the Desktop dialog box (Figure 8.17). A drawing that covers the desktop is called a **wallpaper**.

Figure 8.16

Desktop pattern

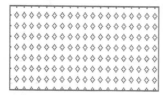

Desktop Patterns. Desktop patterns are strictly optional; they serve no purpose other than to add interest to your windows display. If you wish, you can use a pattern that comes with Windows, edit one of these patterns, or create your own custom pattern. Now you will see what your screen looks like with a different desktop.

EXERCISE 8 . 4   CHANGING THE BACKGROUND PATTERN

1. Double-click on the Desktop icon from the Control Panel. The Desktop dialog box appears as shown in Figure 8.17.

2. Select the Boxes pattern:

  a. Click on the down arrow to the right of the Pattern Name drop-down list box to display a list of stored patterns.

  b. Click on the pattern you would like to use. In this case, click on Boxes.

Figure 8.17

Desktop dialog box

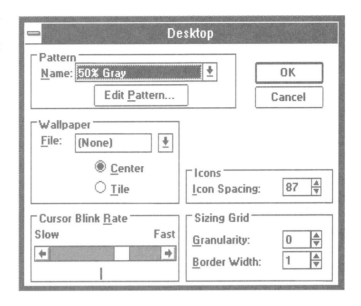

3. Click on the OK command button.

4. Repeat steps 2 and 3 until you have a desktop pattern you like.

Figure 8.18

Desktop Wallpaper

Desktop Wallpaper. The Desktop Wallpaper option allows you to place drawings (graphic files) on the desktop background. You can select from the graphic files that come with the Windows program, or you can create your own. Any bitmapped (.BMP) graphic file can be used as a wallpaper. A wallpaper can be centered on the desktop, as in Figure 8.18, or it can be tiled to fill the entire desktop.

EXERCISE 8 • 5 CHANGING THE DESKTOP WALLPAPER

1. Double-click on the Desktop icon.

2. Click the down arrow in the Wallpaper drop-down file list box to display a list of available graphic files.

3. Click on the PARTY.BMP file. By default, Windows centers the wallpaper file (the Center button is highlighted). Accept this default.

4. Click on the OK command button to "hang" the wallpaper. (See Figure 8.18).

NOTE: You may need to minimize all of the icons on your screen in order to see the wallpaper.

Notice that the wallpaper is centered on the desktop. If you have selected a pattern, the pattern fills the area of the desktop not covered by the wallpaper. Now let's see what the wallpaper would look like if it were tiled to fill the desktop area.

5. Tile the wallpaper so as to fill the desktop area:

   a. Click the down arrow button in the Wallpaper drop-down file list box. The PARTY.BMP file should be selected.

   b. Click on the Tile option button to select it.

   c. Click on the OK command button to "hang" the wallpaper.

The wallpaper now covers the desktop. If you look closely at the desktop, you will see that the graphic has been duplicated enough times to fill the area.

EXERCISE 8 • 6   USING A CUSTOM DESKTOP WALLPAPER

This exercise will use the GRAPHIC.BMP file you created in Session 7 and saved on your *Quick Start* disk. Before you begin this exercise, be sure your *Quick Start* disk is in the appropriate disk drive.

1. Click on the Desktop icon to open the application.

2. Click an insertion point in the Wallpaper file text box and key the filename *A:GRAPHIC.BMP*.

3. Click on the Center option button to select it.

4. Click on the OK command button to "hang" the wallpaper.

Notice that the wallpaper is centered on the desktop. If you have selected a pattern, the pattern fills the area of the desktop not covered by the wallpaper.

5. Reset the wallpaper to none.

   a. Click on the Desktop icon to open the application.

   b. Click the down arrow button in the Wallpaper drop-down file list box and select None.

   c. Click on the OK command button.

Keep in mind that the wallpaper background takes up memory. If you want to use your computer's memory to its best advantage, do not use a wallpaper desktop.

Other Desktop Custom Options. The Desktop dialog box allows you to customize three additional desktop features: the cursor blink rate, the icon spacing, and the sizing grid.

Cursor Blink Rate. The cursor blink rate option adjusts the speed at which the cursor blinks. The cursor blink rate has no effect on the operations of any Windows program; it is an individual preference.

Icon Spacing. The icon spacing feature regulates how closely icons will be placed together. If they tend to overlap, change the spacing by indicating the number of pixels (screen dots) of separation you want between icons. Enter the number in the Icon Spacing text box.

Sizing Grid. The sizing grid has two features: **granularity** and **border width**. The Granularity creates a grid of guidelines that are used to align your desktop elements. It helps align the objects on your desktop more easily by turning on an invisible grid of lines. To use this feature, click the up arrow in the Granularity text box once so that it displays a value of 1, and then choose OK to activate the invisible grid. Selecting a value of 0 will turn off the granularity grid completely.

Window borders can be enlarged or reduced to make more or less room for your desktop. To use the Border Width feature, click on the up or down arrows in the Border Width text box in the Desktop dialog box.

VIEW 2
CHANGING PRINTER SETTINGS

PREVIEW

The hardware settings you are most likely to change are the printer settings. Changing a printer setting may be as simple as selecting from a list of available printers, or it may be as complex as installing a new printer driver—software that tells Windows how to work with a family of printers (you can then select a specific printer model from the driver).

Printer drivers are available on the Windows program disk, on a disk from your dealer, or on a disk from the printer manufacturer. Since you must have the correct printer drivers to install new printers, we will limit the discussion of changing printer settings to selecting the active and default printers.

Selecting the Active and Default Printers

Windows provides a Printers icon for choosing a printer and for changing the settings on those printers already installed. Double-click on the Printers icon on the Control Panel to bring up a Printers dialog box (similar to the one shown in Figure 8.19), which lists all the printers installed in your Windows program.

Figure 8.19

Printers dialog box

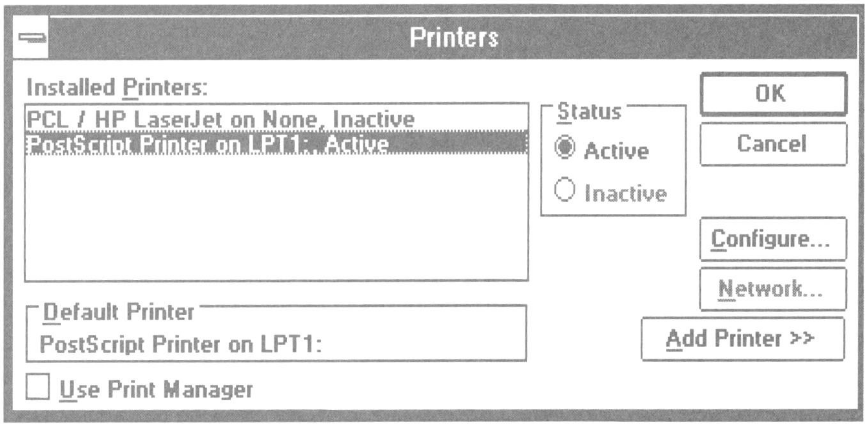

Selecting the Active Printer. As you see in Figure 8.19, Windows can have multiple printers connected to your computer. However, only one printer can be active at a time. To make an inactive printer active, you must make a printer setting change, as follows: First, select the printer you wish to make the active printer; then click on the Active option button in the Status box. The formerly active printer becomes inactive.

EXERCISE 8 • 7　SELECTING THE ACTIVE PRINTER

1. Double-click on the Printers icon to display the Printers dialog box.
2. Click on the printer you wish to make the active printer. (If you have only one printer, click on this printer—it won't change anything, but you'll see how the process works.)
3. Click on the Active option button.
4. Click on the OK command button.

Changing the Default Printer. Windows will automatically use one printer it calls the default printer. If you need to use a printer different from the default printer, you must change the printer settings. To change the default printer, double-click on the printer name in the Printers list box.

EXERCISE 8 • 8　CHANGING THE DEFAULT PRINTER

1. Double-click on the Printers icon to display the Printers dialog box.
2. Double-click on the printer you wish to make the default printer.
3. Click on the OK command button.

NOTE:　Before you leave this session, be sure to return the default printer setting to its original setting.

4. Change the default printer to the original printer by following steps *1* through *3* above.
5. Double-click on the Control-Menu box on the Control Panel.
6. Exit Windows.

The Control Panel allows you to modify your Windows environment in many other ways. Become familiar with the power of the Control Panel so that you can customize the display colors, fonts, icon placement, and desktop layout whenever you work with Windows.

SUMMARY

In this session you learned how to use the Control Panel, which provides different capabilities than most of the other Windows applications. The Control Panel allows you to customize Windows by changing the default settings, the settings originally set by the software developer. Windows provides a desktop environment complete with sound and color, but only with the Control Panel can you change this environment.

The Control Panel gives you an easy way to: modify the sound of the warning beep, change the color of your desktop workspace, remove fonts for your screen and printer, add printers and other communicating devices to your computer, increase or decrease the speed of your mouse, change your background display by adding patterns or pictures to it, add or remove a printer or change its setup, adapt your keyboard to foreign languages, and much more. The Control Panel does indeed let you *control* your environment!

APPENDIX

WINDOWS 3 KEYBOARD SHORTCUTS

WINDOWS 3 KEYBOARD SHORTCUTS

DIALOG BOX

To...	Press...
Cancel All But Active	**Ctrl + [\]**
Exit Box Without Selecting	**[Esc]** or **[Alt] + [F4]**
Move Between Items	**[Tab]** or **[Shift] + [Tab]**
Move to First Item	**[Home]**
Move to Last Item	**[End]**
Move to Beginning of Line	**[Shift] + [Home]**
Move to End of Line	**[Shift] + [End]**
Open a Drop-down List Box	**[Alt] + [Down Arrow]**
Select an Item in a Box	**[Spacebar]**
Select a Check Box	**[Spacebar]**
Select All Items in Box	**[Ctrl] + [/]**
Select an Active Command Button	**[Enter]**

Write

WRITE

To...	Press...
Delete	**[Del]**
Cut	**[Shift] + [Del]**
Copy	**[Ctrl] + [Ins]**
Paste	**[Shift] + [Ins]**
Undo	**[Alt] + [Backspace]**
Move to Next Line	**[Down Arrow]**
Move to Previous Line	**[Up Arrow]**
Move to Next Word	**[Ctrl] + [Right Arrow]**
Move to Previous Word	**[Ctrl] + [Left Arrow]**
Move to Beginning of Line	**[Home]**
Move to End of Line	**[End]**
Move to Beginning of Document	**[Ctrl] + [Home]**

Move to End of Document	**[Ctrl] + [End]**
Move to Previous Screen	**[Pg Up]**
Move to Next Screen	**[Pg Dn]**
Selects Header/Footer	**[Alt] + [F6]**
Find Next Occurrence	**[F3]**
Replace Last Find	**[F3]**
Jump to Specific Page	**[F4]**
Select Normal Style	**[F5]**
Bold Character/Text	**[Ctrl] + [B]**
Italic Character/Text	**[Ctrl] + [I]**
Underline Character/Text	**[Ctrl] + [U]**
Optional Hyphen	**[Ctrl] + [Shift] + [Hyphen]**
Page Break-manual Insert	**[Ctrl] + [Enter]**

To highlight. . .	*Press. . .*
to Next Line	**[Shift] + [Down Arrow]**
to Previous Line	**[Shift] + [Up Arrow]**
to Next Word	**[Ctrl] + [Shift] + [Right Arrow]**
to Previous Word	**[Ctrl] + [Shift] + [Left Arrow]**
to Beginning of Document	**[Ctrl] + [Shift] + [Home]**
to End of Document	**[Ctrl] + [Shift] + [End]**
to Previous Screen	**[Shift] + [Pg Up]**
to Next Screen	**[Shift] + [Pg Dn]**

Program Manager

PROGRAM MANAGER

To. . .	*Press. . .*
Open File	**[Enter]**
Delete File	**[Del]**
Cascade Windows	**[Shift] + [F5]**
Tile Windows	**[Shift] + [F4]**
Get Help	**[Alt] + [H]**
Move Between Group Window	**[Ctrl] + [F6]** or **[Ctrl] + [Tab]**
Start a Highlighted Icon	**[Enter]**
Close a Group Window	**[Ctrl] + [F4]**
Exit from Program Manager	**[Alt] + [F4]**

File Manager

FILE MANAGER

To. . .	*Press. . .*
Get Help on File Manager	**[Alt] + [H]**
Open Directory/File	**[Enter]**
Copy File	**[F8]**
Move File	**[F7]**
Delete	**[Del]**
Select All	**[Ctrl] + [/]**
Deselect All	**[Ctrl] + [\ ]**
Cascade Window	**[Shift] + [F5]**
Tile Window	**[Shift] + [F4]**
Refresh Window	**[F5]**
Expand One Level Tree	**[+]**
Expand Branch Tree	**[*]**
Expand All of Tree	**[Ctrl] + [*]**
Collapse Branch of Tree	**[-]**

Paintbrush

PAINTBRUSH

To. . .	*Press. . .*
Create New File	**[Ctrl] + [N]**
Save File	**[Ctrl] + [S]**
Cut	**[Shift] + [Del]**
Paste	**[Shift] + [Ins]**
Copy	**[Ctrl] + [Ins]**
Undo	**[Alt] + [Backspace]**
View Picture	**[Ctrl] + [C]**
Zoom In	**[Ctrl] + [Z]**
Zoom Out	**[Ctrl] + [O]**
Bold	**[Ctrl] + [B]**
Underline	**[Ctrl] + [U]**
Italic	**[Ctrl] + [I]**

Calendar

CALENDAR

To. . .	Press. . .
Move to Previous Day	[Ctrl] + [Pg Up]
Move to Next Day	[Ctrl] + [Pg Dn]
Show Date	[F4]
Set Alarm	[F5]
Mark Day	[F6]
Set Special Time	[F7]
Change to Day View	[F8]
Change to Month View	[F9]

Cardfile

CARDFILE

To. . .	Press. . .
Find Next Text	[F3]
Go to a Card	[F4]
Autodial	[F5]
Edit Index Line	[F6]
Add Card	[F7]

Notepad

NOTEPAD

To. . .	Press. . .
Find Next Text	[F3]
Display Time/Day	[F5]

INDEX